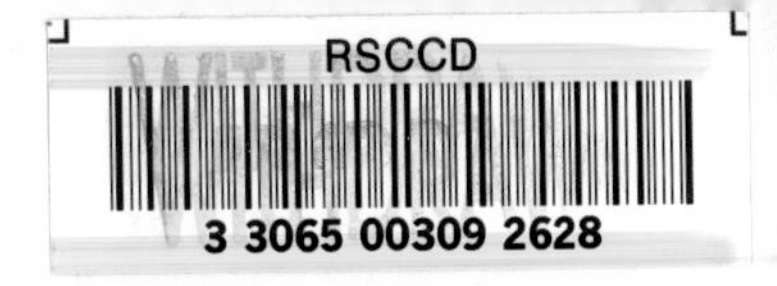

Targets of Opportunity

Targets of Opportunity

On the Militarization of Thinking

SAMUEL WEBER

Fordham University Press ▪ New York ▪ 2005

Library of Congress Cataloging-in-Publication Data

Weber, Samuel, 1940–
Targets of opportunity : on the militarization of thinking / Samuel Weber.—1st ed.
p. cm.
Includes bibliographical references and index.
ISBN 0-8232-2475-9 (hardcover)—ISBN 0-8232-2476-7 (pbk.)
1. Philosophy. 2. War (Philosophy) 3. Psychoanalysis and philosophy.
I. Title.
B105.W3W43 2005
303.6′6—dc22 2005000953

Printed in the United States of America
07 06 05 5 4 3 2 1
First edition

Contents

Preface

Although the history of words is rarely simple or transparent, it is almost always symptomatic, which is to say, significant, though often in a dissimulating mode. That seems especially so for the word around which the following essays revolve: *target.* According to the *OED,* which itself acknowledges an element of uncertainty, the word probably comes from one common to several European languages, including Old Norse, Old English, and Old French: *targa,* meaning "shield." Even when one adds that the kind of shield the word designated was a light and portable one, carried by archers, a connection is suggested that is not necessarily obvious: the "target" is initially a protective "shield." From this to a notion of "targeting" that would emphasize its defensive origins, there is a considerable leap. And yet, independently of the etymology of the word, the steady increase in popularity of the term, in particular, its extension from what was initially only a noun to a verb, would take on quite a different significance were the force driving it linked to a sense of danger, to feelings of anxiety and fear, and to the desire to protect and secure. This link between what was originally a protective shield and an activity that seeks to "hit" or "seize" control of a more or less distant object acquires greater import when one considers the long-standing function of "targeting" as a metaphor or figure for thinking itself—that is, for what philosophers, from the scholastics to Husserlian phenomenology, have designated as "intentionality," which, in the modern period at least, has been employed to define the structure of consciousness. If consciousness is understood as consciousness "of an object," the manner in which it negotiates the distance that separates it from its object is often compared to an archer taking aim at an object: in short, to "targeting." With the following difference: the root of *intention* is *tension*, related both to "tending" and to "holding"; this emphasizes the effort required to overcome distance in achieving one's aims or ends. Such an effort, and the consequent tension it implies, tend to disappear when the goal is designated by the same word as the attempt to reach it.

An example: In Plato's dialogue known as the "Lesser Hippias," Socrates subjects Hippias to the following interrogation:

> *Socrates.* And is it better to possess the mind of an archer who voluntarily or involuntarily misses the mark [*hamartanei*]?
> *Hippias.* Of him who voluntarily misses.
> *Socrates.* This would be the better mind for the purposes of archery?
> *Hippias.* Yes.
> *Socrates.* Then the mind which involuntarily errs is worse than the mind which errs voluntarily?
> *Hippias.* Yes, certainly, in the use of the bow.
> *Socrates.* And will our minds be better if they do wrong and make mistakes voluntarily, or involuntarily? (375b ff.)[1]

The activity of the mind, thinking, is thus construed on the model of the archer hitting—or missing, voluntarily or not—the mark. Thinking is hitting the mark, making the point: targeting.

Even against the background of this massive and long-standing tradition, however, a certain inflation seems to have marked the use of the word *target-targeting* in the past decades, at least in the version of English with which I am familiar: American English. An Internet search using the word *targeting* takes Google all of 0.24 seconds to come up with 3,860,000 occurrences. These include *The Journal of Targeting, Measurement and Analysis for Marketing*, "Al Qaeda again targeting New York," "How Spammers are targeting Blogs," and "Advanced Targeting Systems," which identifies itself as a "Biotechnology company dedicated to providing quality targeting reagents: immunotoxins, targeted toxins."

What, if anything, does this inflation in the use of the words *target* and *targeting* tell us about the world in which we are living and the direction in which it is going? This question was posed at the outbreak of the second war against Iraq, when the term *target of opportunity* surfaced to describe the reason why the American military jumped the gun by destroying a house in Baghdad where Saddam Hussein was thought to be at the time. Since I myself had, in a somewhat different context, been a "target of opportunity" appointment, I was compelled to reflect upon a situation in which the same term could acquire such diverse meanings.

When this occurred, I was already involved in a series of studies concerning the representation of violence on television, on the one hand, and in certain "theoretical" texts, on the other. The response of the American government to the attacks of September 11, 2001, in particular its endorsement and practice of preventive, or "preemptive" military intervention, although by no means entirely unprecedented in the history of American foreign policy, added a sense of urgency to the project, which, to be sure, is not primarily directed at political events or processes. Rather, it seeks to explore, in the most unsystematic manner imaginable, certain aspects of what might constitute part of the "background" and indirect history of those events: the ramifications of "targeting" in its literal and figurative manifestations.

The result is a patchwork of readings and a series of unanswered questions concerning the relation of "targeting" to thinking, political action, and self-definition. Although targeting is generally approached with a certain suspicion in these readings, it is also clear that it is not something that can simply be "done away with," a problem I discuss in more detail in regard to Freud's staging of "The Man Moses" (Chapter 4). On the contrary, "targeting" seems inextricable from thinking, at least where its aim—its target?—is defined in cognitive terms, as it is in these essays. This is perhaps why, in the final chapter, it is in a reading of poetry—Benjamin's reading of two poems by Hölderlin—that a possible alternative emerges to the kind of movement otherwise encountered in this book.

If one could sketch a figural trajectory of these essays, it would thus lead from the *target*, through the *network*, to a different kind of *netting*, and ultimately not to a figure in the carpet but rather to a figure *of carpets*, upon which footsteps leave traces. Whether such carpets and traces provide a thinkable alternative to the more lethal kind of targeting with which we are becoming increasingly familiar is a question that the readers of these essays are asked to confront.

Targets of Opportunity

CHAPTER

1

"A Rather Singular Strike"

> Less than a day after the attacks [on September 11, 2001], Donald H. Rumsfeld, the secretary of defense, said at a cabinet-level meeting that "there were no decent targets for bombing in Afghanistan and that we should consider bombing Iraq" instead because it had "better targets."
>
> —*New York Times*, March 22, 2004

> The unfolding Spanish investigation has shown that the terrorists continue to exploit a tactical advantage. The militants operate in an ever-changing constellation of cells, moving freely from country to country across the continent, guided by opportunity and fanaticism.
>
> —*New York Times*, March 22, 2004

Shortly before 4 P.M. on March 19, 2003, the director of the CIA, George Tenet, met with President George W. Bush and his closest advisors in order to inform them of a new and potentially important discovery. Preparation for the invasion of Iraq had almost been concluded, and the start of military action was at the most days away. Director Tenet informed the president and his staff that the CIA had received reliable and precise information concerning the whereabouts of Saddam Hussein. The Iraqi president and many of his senior collaborators were gathered in a villa in southern Baghdad that night, whose address was known to the CIA. A story in the *Washington Post* described the information Tenet conveyed to his political superiors as both "unforeseen and perishable."[1] The story ran under the headline "'Target of Opportunity' Seized," in which the phrase *target of opportunity* was set in quotes. An unforeseen event—precise information concerning the whereabouts of Saddam Hussein and his advisors—had arisen and a decision had to be made rapidly if this information was to be successfully exploited. After three hours of discussion, at roughly 6:30 P.M., the President of the United States signed a command authorizing the air force to destroy the "anonymous house in Baghdad" as quickly as possible. A few hours later, at 3:33 A.M. local time, the first bombs and missiles were launched; full-fledged military action against Iraq began shortly thereafter. As we now know, although the immediate target was destroyed, the opportunity was missed, since the major target escaped, to be captured only many months later.

In order to seize the opportunity that apparently presented itself on March 19, the American war plan had to be modified, and the start of hostilities advanced by at least twenty-four hours. As one unnamed American official quoted in the *Post* article put it: "If you're going to take a shot like this, you're going to take a shot at the top guy. . . . It was a fairly singular strike."

The "strike" was "fairly singular" in more than one sense. Most obviously, it was "fairly singular" in seeking to decapitate the "top guy" and with him a good part of the Iraqi leadership at the very outset, in the hope of thereby winning the war before it had to be fought on the ground. But quite apart from its specific target, the opportunity was "fairly singular" in its formal properties. First, as the *Post* story reported, it was based on "intelligence [that] was unforeseen and perishable, presenting what one administration official called 'a target of opportunity' that might not come again." The "target" that thus presented itself was "opportune" in the sense of being present—literally, a gateway (portal) that would "open" only for a brief span of time. Indeed, one could say that it had a brief "lifetime" or, perhaps more in synch with current American parlance, a short "shelf-life." Its singularity consisted first, and perhaps foremost, in its thus emerging "unforeseen" and briefly. It is perhaps neither entirely insignificant nor simply ironic to note that this essentially temporal dimension of the event was designated in the *Post* story as "perishable." To seize this opportunity before it "perished"—that is, passed away irrevocably, as though it were mortal—would entail putting an end to many human lives. Seizing not just the "opportunity" but the "target of opportunity"—the opportunity *as* target—would thus entail exploiting the mortality of the target, presumably to further the cause of those doing the targeting. A fleeting opportunity would thus be transformed or transfigured into a portal or passageway to survival and security, very much in the spirit of the "war on terror" and for "freedom." But if "terror" was identified as the enemy, in what did its threat consist? And if freedom was the goal, then *from* what or *to* what end?

The "fairly singular strike" was by no means the first of its kind, nor would it be the last. But although it had predecessors, it was not simply a repetition of the same, as the *Washington Post* story reminded its readers: "The 1991 Persian Gulf War included hundreds of strikes at 'leadership targets,' but President George H. W. Bush and his advisors did not acknowledge they were aimed at Saddam specifically."[2] A decade later this scruple no longer obtained. A major, determining difference, of course, was "September 11" and the ensuing "war on terror." Initially given the face and name of Osama bin Laden, leader of Al-Qaeda, the focus rapidly shifted to the Iraqi head of state. The indeterminate nebulousness of "terror" required a human face and name in order not just to be made real for a larger public but to be identified as the enemy—the object—of a war presented not primarily as one between ideologies, states, or even empires, but rather as a cultural, religious, and ultimately moral conflict between Freedom and Justice on one side, and Terror and Evil on the other: "good guys" (us) versus "bad guys" (them); Manichaeism meets Star Wars.

This in turn made it clear that, however different the war on terror was going to be from traditional wars, with their relatively well-defined enemies, it would still involve one of the basic mechanisms of traditional hunting and combat, in however modified and modernized a form: namely, "targeting." The enemy would have to be *identified* and *localized*, *named* and *depicted*, in order to be made into an accessible target, susceptible of destruction. None of this was, per se, entirely new. What *was*, however, was the mobility, indeterminate structure, and unpredictability of the spatio-temporal *medium* in which such targets had to be sited. One of the results of this situation was that time had increasingly to be factored into the process of targeting. Targets thus became ever more a function of "opportunity," and the effective "seizing" of opportunity increasingly a condition for successful targeting. In theaters of conflict that had become highly mobile and changeable, "targets" and "opportunity" were linked as never before.

Yet the phrase itself, in a military sense, already had a long history, going back at least as far as the Second World War. It is probably not fortuitous that the earliest documented use I have found relates to the most mobile component of the military, the air force, and in particular to instructions given American pilots, who, after striking their assigned targets, were encouraged to look for "targets of opportunity," that is, targets that were not foreseen or planned.[3] But if the origin of the phrase was initially military, over the past decades the scope of its usage has expanded drastically. Most academics will be familiar with the notion as designating a particular form of recruitment, designed either to correct imbalances in group representation or to attract individuals of unusual qualifications who do not necessarily fit the traditional desiderata of discipline-oriented departments. While this use of the phrase seems largely limited to universities in the United States, there is another area of scientific research in which the term is employed internationally: in astrophysics, where the phrase has acquired a slightly different acronym. There it is no longer known as a TOP, as in American academia, but as a TOO, for reasons that are immediately related to its specific function. It designates a process by which scientists apply to use equipment, in particular, telescopes, independently of the established schedule, in order to be able to observe unforeseen events of limited duration that otherwise could not be investigated. If granted, the investigator thus preempts the regular scheduling, which perhaps explains why this form of "target of opportunity" should be abbreviated as TOO rather than as TOP, as in "excellence."

What all these very different uses of the phrase have in common is the effort to recognize and *respond* to an event that is sufficiently *singular* to resist subsumption under established rules and procedures. To be effective, the response to the singular and unpredictable event tends to suspend or alter established plans, procedures, or schedules. If the latter seek to organize and regularize spatio-temporal events in terms of their predictability, the unpredictable requires the suspension or alteration of the established grid. The very singularity of a "target of opportunity" thus presupposes the *generality* of an established order, scheme, organization, or plan, in respect to which an event defines itself as exceptional or extraordinary. The determination of such an event as a "target," however, implies an effort on the part of the system to integrate or appropriate the singularity of the event through an equally exceptional response. Given that the event's singularity is generally determined with respect to its nonpermanence and nonubiquity, the response generally has to be "rapid" and "focused" if it is to be effective. This in turn implies that time and space are to be transformed from media of alteration and dislocation into conditions of self-fulfillment and appropriation. In this respect, the term *target of opportunity* is related to another common phrase, *window of opportunity*, as implementation is to potentiality. Insofar, however, as implementation depends not just upon identifying and responding to a "target of opportunity" but upon controlling access to it, realization in this situation entails a particular sort of "de-realization": once the event is defined as a "target," it is treated as though it were localizable and controllable, either through integration, as in academia (TOP: target of opportunity recruitments), or through disintegration, as in the military sense: the target is hit and destroyed. Mediating between these two poles of the alternative integrate-disintegrate is the astrophysical TOO, since it also "aims" to appropriate the singular event through the use of telescopes that neutralize distance (tele-) and transience by transforming "chance" into an "opportunity" for the production of "knowledge." Insofar as such knowledge, in conformity with the defining criterion of validity or of truth, is generally held to be relatively impervious to spatio-temporal alteration, the TOO implies a certain overcoming of the limitations of finitude. Such overcoming does not entail personal immortality, to be sure, but it does promise a certain kind of survival: that of the generalized process of knowledge production and reception to which such "targeting" both belongs, and contributes.

It is probably no accident that the technology of observing at a distance, that of the telescope, is associated with the scientific targeting of opportunity: the TOO. In the Western tradition, at least, the faculty of vision has been most closely associated with the constitution of knowledge and hence with its power to overcome distance and assimilate alterity. The configuration of knowledge, vision, targeting, and survival has a long history. In this connection, a Greek terminological distinction recalled by Jean-Luc Nancy in an early essay is illuminating with respect to the prehistory of "targeting":

> There are two concepts of the end—or, rather, doubtless the end itself does not cease dividing itself in accordance with two concepts: *skopos* and *telos* (the Stoics were familiar with this distinction). *Skopos* is the target [*la cible*] that one has in one's sights and at which one takes aim; it is the goal presently and clearly offered to an intention [*une visée*]. *Telos*, by contrast, is the fulfillment of an action or of a process, its development up to its end (e.g., the fruit is not the target of the tree, any more than the target is the fruit of the archer). Thus the *telos* can also designate the summit, the apex, or, again, the supreme power or sovereign jurisdiction. . . . *Skopos* is the draw of the bow, *telos*, life and death.[4]

Nancy's interpretation of the distinction between *skopos* and *telos* brings out a number of important points and also raises certain questions. It emphasizes the privileged relation between "targeting," "aiming," and sighting. *Skopos* is already, tendentially, the *tele-scope,* since "the one who aims" is also "the one who surveys." To survey, in this sense, is to command at a distance.

And commanding involves not just the demonstration or exercise of power as such but a very specific use of it: namely, that of "keeping" and "protecting"—the one who surveys is also the one who keeps and protects (*qui garde*). To be able to survey in order to take aim implies a position situated above the fray, as it were, as a "master" or a "protector." According to Liddell-Scott, this is said of "gods and kings" (Pindar), but also of more human watchmen and guards, "look-outs," spies, and scouts. At the same time, as Nancy writes, *skopos* designates not just the act but also the object of such watching: the mark or target. It is as if the *word*, in designating both object and subject, both the target and the targeting, had itself already semantically overcome the distance and the difference in the process it designates.

Nancy describes the distinction between *skopos* and *telos* as a self-bifurcation of the notion of *end* (in the dual sense of termination and consummation). Having established this, he goes on to develop a notion of *telos* freed, as it were, from its scopic shadow. *Skopos* functions, in his argument at least, primarily as a backdrop against which to set off the luster of *telos*, as defining a relation that is ultimately internal, "entelechical": "The *telos,* in a certain way, is more entelechical than teleological" (41). By contrast *skopos* is said to presuppose the external and prior givenness of its target, "a model given in advance, an original to be rejoined or recovered" (42).

And yet the very fact that the word *skopos* designates both subject and object, both archer and target, would seem to introduce an element of instability into this ontological, mimetological presupposition of a pregiven, self-present original. This aspect becomes more manifest, of course, where it is a question not just of targets but of targets of *opportunity,* which is to say, where time and space are decisive factors in the establishment of the target. Even without this explicit reference to spatio-temporal localization, it is difficult to conceive how a "target" could be construed simply as self-contained or self-present. What is involved here is the difference between something simply being "seen" and something being "sighted"—that is, discovered, localized, identified in order to be hit or struck. Nancy emphasizes that the *telos* entails the relation of "life and death" as well as the existential "development" of something to its utmost limit, "beyond which there is no longer anything that this thing could still become" (41). But what if the banal *tir à l'arc* and the activity it permits—in short, what if *skopos* itself were experienced as just such a limit experience? What if the enabling limits associated with the *telos* were themselves made dependent upon the power to treat the other as *skopos*: target and targeter? What would this signify for an end that defined its *telos*—its *task*[5]—precisely as that of becoming a *skopos*? What sort of "self" would be implied by such a bifurcation, and what sort of "ends" would it entail?

Philosophers have generally tended to privilege questions of *telos* over those of *skopos*. Indeed, the word *skopos* is rarely to be found among vocabularies of Greek philosophy, in sharp contrast to *telos*, one of its master words. If we want, therefore, to explore the implications of *skopos* and its attendant, and perhaps originating verb, *skeptomai,* we will have to look elsewhere, to other sorts of texts—mindful of the fact that in so doing we inevitably perform one of the activities designated by the verb *skeptomai*: to consider, examine, watch out for.

With these questions in mind, let us turn to one of the most famous or infamous scenes of Greek literature, Book 22 of the *Odyssey,* where the hero, having finally returned home, prepares the fate of the suitors:

> Shedding his rags, the indomitable Odysseus leapt onto the great threshold, holding his bow and his quiver full of arrows. Spreading the quick arrows at his feet, he called to the suitors: "That 'harmless game' is done! Now there is another target! No man has hit it yet; let's see if with Apollo's help the glory can be mine." With that, he let fly the bitter arrow at Antinous, who was about to raise his

> beautiful, dual-handled golden goblet to take a drink. Bloodshed was not in his thoughts; who could imagine at the festal board that one man amongst many, even a very strong one, would bring certain death upon him? Yet Odysseus shot the arrow and struck him in the throat; the point ran through the soft neck. Dropping the cup as he was hit, Antinous lurched to one side. A thick jet of blood gushed from his nostrils; his foot lashed out and kicked the table from him, spilling all the food on the ground, and his bread and meat were smeared with gore.
>
> Then a great uproar spread all through the place. Seeing the man fall, the suitors leapt up from their seats in excitement and looked all round at the walls, but there was neither shield nor spear to be seen. . . . Poor fools! They did not know that the coils of death were made fast about them all. (*Odyssey*, 22:1–35[6])

Perhaps the first great revenge massacre in Western literature—in any event, surely the most memorable—this scene of violence has acquired a strange resonance today. Violence, lovingly depicted in detail, becomes almost a source of enjoyment by virtue of its context: in the *Odyssey*, that of the hero reclaiming what is rightfully his: his home, wife, and family, all of which have been thoroughly abused by the suitors in the twenty years of his absence. Odysseus understands his violence to be punishment and retribution, as well as a means of recovering what has been taken from him. The few who remained loyal to him in his absence are spared, the others dispatched.

But this moral justification is required because of a very different and problematic convergence: that of *violence done to others* as the condition for the *recovery and fulfillment of self*. Of course, the self-concerned, however heroic, is by no means autonomous in the modern sense and is constantly depicted as dependent upon the immortal gods. But, as Zeus makes explicit at the very beginning of the *Odyssey*, such dependence does not absolve human beings of responsibility and a certain freedom: "How lamentable that men should blame the gods and regard *us* as the source of their troubles, when it is their own wickedness that brings them sufferings worse than any destiny allots them" (*Odyssey*, 1:32–35).

Precisely the fact of being responsible for one's fate in a situation of nonautonomy defines the initial designation of Odysseus as a "polytrope," one who is able to respond to and exploit the many twists and turns of fate to which he is exposed. But all of these vicissitudes are negotiated in view of the ultimate recuperation of his property: wife, house, family, and, perhaps above all, dignity (*timē*). What from our perspective is significant, however, is that this culminating retrieval is achieved and consummated through a deadly practice of targeting. To be successful, careful preparation is required. Apart from secrecy and disguise, which insure that the attack comes as a complete surprise to its victims, Odysseus prepares his revenge by taking a number of preliminary steps. First and probably foremost, he demands and receives from Zeus a double portent as confirmation that his project has divine approval (*Odyssey*, 20:97–120). This is in sharp contrast to the suitors, who in their revels ignore a growing number of signs of approaching disaster. Second, once he has decided to attempt his revenge, he has Telemachus remove all weapons and shields from the great hall where the suitors are gathered, so that they will be defenseless when he attacks (*Odyssey*, 19:5–10). Third, he instructs Eumaeus, the cowherd, to bring him the great bow, which will serve as his weapon of revenge. Fourth, he assigns to Philoetius, the swineherd, the task "of bolting and roping the courtyard gate" (*Odyssey*, 21:240–41), so that the suitors will be trapped in the hall.

Notwithstanding all this careful planning, success depends upon a factor that Odysseus cannot entirely control: on the fortuitous temporal convergence of the festival dedicated to Apollo, "the glorious archer" (*Odyssey*, 21:266), with Penelope's scheme to organize a competition among the suitors in emulation of Odysseus, who, she reminds them, with his great bow would send a single arrow through twelve axe handles, aligned one behind the other (*Odyssey*, 19:570–80). If any suitor can accomplish this feat, Penelope will consent to be his wife.

This "harmless game" of archery (in the words of Antinous), taking place on the day of the festival in honor of the divine archer, Apollo, constitutes the "opportunity" that Odysseus is quick to recognize and seize. Indeed, when Penelope first tells him of her project with the bow, his response reflects his sense of urgency in recognizing a unique opportunity: "Worthy spouse of Laertes' son, Odysseus, do not put off [more literally, throw back: *meketi nun anaballē*, *Odyssey*, 19:584] in your house the competition, start it now." The opportunity consists in the convergence of festival and competition.

Thus the scene is set for what at first looks like a relatively "anodyne game" of archery, but serves both as the condition and as the model of the slaughter to come.[7] It is a model insofar as it demonstrates that the suitors lack the force necessary to bend the bow, much less hit the mark, and it is the condition that allows Odysseus to "turn" the game into the deadly shooting match. The "game" is also a model in another sense, for it exhibits the power of targeting over targets: twelve axes are pierced by a single arrow. The detailed account of this feat reveals just how much the act of targeting transcends in significance its merely instrumental value—precisely by comparing the "bow" in the hands of Odysseus to a kind of musical instrument:

> Odysseus now had the bow in his hands and was twisting it about, testing it this way and that, for fear that the worms might have eaten into the horn in the long absence of the owner. . . . Amid all the banter [of the suitors], cool-headed Odysseus poised the great bow and gave it a final inspection. And now, as easily as a musician who knows his lyre strings the cord on a new peg after looping the twisted sheep-gut at both ends, he strung the great bow without effort or haste and with his right hand proved the string, which gave a lovely sound in answer like a swallow's note. . . .
>
> One arrow lay exposed on the table beside him; the rest, which the Achaean lords were soon to feel, being still inside their hollow quiver. He picked up this shaft, set it

> against the bridge of the bow, drew back the grooved end and the string together, all without rising from his stool, and, aiming straight ahead, he shot. Not a single axe did he miss. From one hole to the other, passing through all the hatchets, the arrow with its weighted point exited at the other side, while the hero said to Telemachus: "Did he make you a laughing stock, Telemachus, this guest sitting in your hall? Did I hit the target? And to bend the bow, did I have to struggle too hard? Ah, my force is intact, despite the insults of the suitors. But now the moment has come." (*Odyssey*, 21:392–425)

What, beyond the sound of the cord, is involved in the comparison of Odysseus's handling of the bow, first with a musician handling a lyre, then with a swallow's song? Nothing less, perhaps, than the ability to resist the ravages of time. Odysseus examines the bow carefully to test for such damage, and when he has hit his first target, he confirms that his "force is intact," having withstood the passage of time as the medium of loss and decline. The song of an individual swallow may be ephemeral, but its imitation through a human instrument renders it reproducible at will and indefinitely.

Targeting in general, then, can be seen as a means of overcoming spatial and temporal dislocation, especially with respect to human finitude. This is perhaps nowhere more powerfully at work than where the targeting involves more than just hitting or missing a mark: where it manifests a decision concerning the life and death of the target. The recounting of the death of Antinous, in its attention to detail, mitigates somewhat the sense of merited revenge by preparing it with a meticulous depiction of unsuspecting vulnerability. This time it is not the twelve hatchets that are pierced by the arrow, but Antinous's "soft neck." I repeat the earlier citation:

> Antinous . . . was about to raise his beautiful, dual-handled golden goblet to take a drink. Bloodshed was not in his thoughts; who could imagine at the festal board that one man amongst many, even a very strong one, would bring certain death upon him? Yet Odysseus shot the

> arrow and struck him in the throat; the point ran through the soft neck. Dropping the cup as he was hit, Antinous lurched to one side. A thick jet of blood gushed from his nostrils; his foot lashed out and kicked the table from him, spilling all the food on the ground, and his bread and meat were smeared with gore.

Antinous is taken entirely by surprise, just as he is about to "lift" the "beautiful, dual-handled golden goblet." This intended act is cut short by Odysseus's arrow, which strikes "him in the throat," piercing "the soft neck." Antinous loses control, first of the cup, "dropping [it] as he was hit," and then of his body, as he "lurches to one side." As he drops the goblet, spilling the wine, his body loses its ability to serve as a container—which is to say, to define the separation of self and other, internal and external: "a thick jet of blood gushed from his nostrils." Following the shock, his individual bodily members seem to take on a life of their own. In an involuntary gesture of protest and rejection that is reflexive and utterly out of his conscious control, "his foot lashed out and kicked the table from him, spilling all the food on the ground, and his bread and meat were smeared with gore." This juxtaposition of eating and dying is already announced by Odysseus, who, immediately after hitting the hatchets with the arrow announces that "the time has come now to get . . . supper ready" for the suitors. The arrows that strike their targets are thus not simply a "just dessert" but a lethal nourishment administered by a sovereign who reasserts his power over the life and death of his subjects. His act, however, enhances not the lives of his victims but only his own.

To be sure, the context of the Homeric epic forbids the kind of conclusions that would be appropriate to the modern Western category of autonomous subjectivity. And yet an aura of ritual sacrifice seems to hang over this massacre, which is also presented as an act of purgation: the suitors are slaughtered as they themselves in the many years of his absence slaughtered Odysseus's cattle, not in sacrifice, to be sure, but to feast upon them. This is why it is by no means simply fortuitous that, besides his son, Odysseus's two allies in carrying out his plan are his swineherd and cowherd. The destruction of life—here, that of the suitors—is portrayed as necessary for the reestablishment of orderly and stable conditions of life in Ithaca. But it must not be overlooked that this quid pro quo, which consummates Odysseus's homecoming, does not provide a definitive conclusion to his life. He warns Penelope not to believe that with his return he is "at the end of his trials":

> It still remains for me to conduct to its end, some day, a task that is complicated, difficult, without measure; . . . Tiresias told me to go from town to town carrying in my arms a polished oar until at the end I arrive at people who don't know the sea and never salt their food, who have never seen vessels with purple cheeks, nor polished oars, these wings of ships. . . . On the road, another traveler must ask me why I have that grain shovel on my shining shoulder." (*Odyssey*, 23:265–83)

On that day, Odysseus concludes, he will "plant his oar in the earth" and, after making the appropriate sacrifices to Poseidon and the other gods, finally be able to conclude his life in peace, succumbing only "to the gentlest of deaths, come from the sea, after a happy old age, surrounded by prosperous people" (*Odyssey*, 23:283–85).

Thus all of Odysseus's targeting—the scrupulous preparation, securing the field within which the targets are situated, the "tuning" of the instrument, the actual shooting—all this "scopic" activity does not alter or supplant the "end," which requires very different procedures to be properly attained. The movement toward the *telos* is never linear or goal-directed, but rather involves a deliberate wandering, following the tortuous path indicated by the blind oracle, which will once again lead Odysseus *away* from all that is familiar in search of a very different kind of people, one that does not know the sea and therefore can mistake a polished oar for a ploughshare. But none of this will be depicted in the *Odyssey*, which concludes with the hero's homecoming, but not with the end of his life. It is as if that end remains outside the scope of the narrative.

That Odysseus's targeting does not coincide with the end or ends of his life is underscored by his dependence on the blind seer, Tiresias, whose oracle defines a path that can be anticipated and sought out, but not simply followed as though it led to an aim or a goal. It is a path that cannot be mapped in advance. Indeed, the very success of Odysseus's targeting—and in general, of all his goal-directed activity and planning—depends on his recognition that its *scope* is limited.

But to *acknowledge* such enabling limitation is not equivalent to making it an object of *knowledge*. Precisely the divergence between the two and the challenge of negotiating their interplay is what renders the figure of archery—and, hence, of targeting—a suggestive metaphor for any sort of intentional action or activity, including, above all, that of *judging*. Since, as we have seen, the ostensibly literal use of targeting already entails judgments of various sorts, as well as their implementation through action, it is of particular interest that intentional activity itself is subject to the same vicissitudes that affect the process of targeting. The correspondence theory of truth only strengthens this analogy. Thus in the *Theaetetus* Socrates compares the person who errs to a bad archer who misses the mark:

> *Socrates.* If you know one of two people and also perceive him and if you get the knowledge you have to correspond with the perception of him, you will never think he is another person whom you both know and perceive, if your knowledge of him likewise corresponds with the perception. That is so, isn't it?
>
> *Theaetetus.* Yes.
>
> *Socrates.* But there is left over the case I have been describing now, in which we say false judgment does occur—the possibility that you may know both and see or otherwise perceive both, but not get the two imprints to correspond each with its proper perception. Like a bad archer, you may shoot to one side and miss the mark [*kai hamartein*]—which is indeed another phrase we use for error. (194a)

The correspondence theory of truth, which later will be defined as the *adaequatio intellectus et rei*, presupposes a certain divergence or distance between the thing to be cognized and the thought or representation of it. Otherwise the "co-" of cognition would be unnecessary, since there would be immediate *intuition* of the object. The question here is how the gap between *intellectus* and *re* comes to be bridged, and it is in this context that the figures of archery and of targeting are often invoked. But it is also no accident that, in the passage from the *Thaeatetus* just cited, Socrates invokes this figure in a negative context: to illustrate not "hitting the mark" but rather "missing" it. This is also the form in which it takes on considerable importance in Aristotle's *Poetics,* where, along with *peripeteia* ("reversal") and *anagnōrisis* ("recognition"), it appears, briefly, as the third component of complex tragic plots, the one that explains the other two. If, as Stephen Halliwell observes, "The common premise underlying reversal, recognition and *hamartia* is human ignorance,"[8] his ensuing discussion goes on to show how difficult it is to reduce "human ignorance" to a single common denominator. He thus concludes that the word *hamartia* resists univocal translation into English, and that none of the usual candidates—"error, fault, mistake, flaw"—is fully acceptable. It is as if one of the key words that seeks to designate an effect of human limitation—Halliwell opts for "fallibility" or "failing" as the least inadequate of translations—itself enacts or performs what it also seeks to signify: in English, at least, *hamartia* misses the mark and thus itself remains equivocal and ambiguous. Unless, of course, just such equivocation and ambiguity were the "mark" it seeks to designate: a mark that, precisely because of its lack of unity, will be missed by any attempt to designate it univocally. In which case, a mark so disunited could be "hit" only by being missed, albeit in a certain way: a way that would bring out the *intricate network of meanings* in which every mark, every target is perhaps inevitably inscribed.

The inscription of every single mark in such a relational network would make the success or failure of one's "aiming" depend on factors that transcend the mark as such but also determine it or, one could also say, *localize* it. In Greek, the factor that would situate and supplement *hamartia* in its negative dimension of "failure" or "failing" is designated as *tuchē.* The following, well-known passage describing the different ways of "inflicting harm," from Aristotle's *Nichomachean Ethics,* brings out this relation between *hamartia* and *tuchē*:

> Thus there are three kinds of injury in transactions between man and man; those done in ignorance are *mistakes* [*hamartia*] when the person acted on, the act, the instrument, or the end that will be attained is other than the agent supposed; the agent thought either that he was not hitting anyone or that he was not hitting with this missile or not hitting this person or to this end, but a result followed other than that which he thought likely (e.g., he threw not with intent to wound but only to touch), or the person hit or the missile was other than he supposed. Now when (1) the injury takes place contrary to reasonable expectation, it is a *mishap* [*atuchēma*]. When (2) it is not contrary to reasonable expectation but does not imply vice, it is a *mistake* [*hamartia*] (for a man makes a mistake when the fault originates in him, but is the victim of accident when the origin lies outside him). When (3) he acts with knowledge but not after deliberation, it is an *act of injustice* [*adikia*]. (5.1135b10–19)

Whereas a mistake, *hamartia,* has its causes "within" the doer, the origin of a mishap, *atuchēma,* "lies outside" the agent. If an aim is to attain its goal, hit its mark, it must therefore avoid both internal "error" and external "mishap," and the latter, if not the former, implies a dependence upon external and uncontrollable factors. Describing what he calls "the traditional mentality about the idea of *tuchē*, Halliwell writes that "it represents a source of causation which lies beyond human comprehension or rational expectation."[9] This constitutive opacity renders all the more significant the fact that the noun *tuchē* shares the same root, *tuch-*, as the verb *tuchāno, teuxomai,* meaning "to hit a mark with an arrow." Thus the happy or fortunate meeting of circumstances that is a necessary condition for the success of all aiming is *itself* construed as a kind of hitting the mark—this time, however, not as one that necessarily presupposes a will, desire, or intention, or at least one that can be controlled. If *tuchē* in this sense is a condition of successful targeting, then all such targeting will necessarily entail a certain relation to "opportunity": every target is a target of opportunity.[10]

But this also implies that every target is inscribed in a network or chain of events that inevitably exceeds the opportunity that can be seized or the horizon that can be seen. Missing or hitting the mark thus constitutes only a small part of this overriding and irreducible possibility, for missing or hitting a mark is as such always a singular occurrence, although one that can produce unforeseen aftereffects and ramifications. In short, the bracketing of time and space as media of alteration, or the temporary reduction of their dislocating effects—as when Odysseus seals off the courtyard where the suitors are celebrating—an act that to some extent is an inevitable precondition of focusing upon a target (securing the field of fire), by no means eliminates the power of such aftereffects. Indeed, whereas targeting tends to generalize momentary control of a situation qua opportunity and project it indefinitely upon the future, it can wind up exposing itself all the more destructively to the unforeseen. This seems to be one of the lessons that Thucydides draws in his history of the Peloponnesian War. The Athenians, in their discourse to the Spartans, before the outbreak of hostilities, utter the following warning:

> Consider beforehand how unpredictable a thing is war before you find yourselves engaged in it. Should it prove to be long, the outcome usually depends upon chance occurrences, from whose control we are [on both sides] equally removed, so that how it will end remains a risk in the dark. At the beginning of a war, people first devote themselves to activity [which they ought to do later]. But when they have already experienced some disaster, they cling to thought. (1.78)

H.-P. Stahl glosses this with the following question: "Do the Athenians realize how much this warning applies also to the powerful? The ambiguity and irony of this passage are surely the conscious intention of Thucydides."[11] The speech of the Spartan king, Archidamus, shows that at least some Spartans were well aware of this possibility. The king cautions his countrymen to reflect before rushing into war: "Many wars have I lived through myself, Spartans, and know that those of my generation among you are in the same situation, so that no one will begin this thing out of inexperience, as the crowd might, or out of the idea that it would be a good or sure thing. And this war, over which you are deliberating, will not be the most insignificant one either" (1.80).

Archidamus reviews all the practical questions to be considered: money, above all, but also the political and geopolitical situation, all of which, in his assessment, pose great obstacles to a Spartan victory. No matter how careful the planning, he warns, "We should believe that the calculations of others are similar [to ours] and that circumstances resulting from chance are not [beforehand] susceptible of rational analysis [*tas prospiptousas tuchas ou logo diairetās*)" (1.84). Archidamus counsels prudence: he advises the Spartans to accept the Athenian offer of arbitration, if only to win time for necessary preparations. Only if subsequent negotiations fail should Sparta go to war, after two years of preparation.

Archidamus's words of caution do not carry the day, however, but rather the much shorter and simpler declaration of Sthenelaïdas. Like the king, he starts his discourse with a first-person declaration, but of a very different kind. Addressing not the considerations that the king has just brought forward but rather the arguments of the Athenian emissaries, he dismisses them as follows:

> The many words of the Athenians I do not understand; for in all their self-praise they nowhere contest that they have violated the rights of our allies and of the Peloponnesians. If they once behaved so capably against the Persians and now act so badly against us, they deserve a double punishment, since they have changed so much for the worse. We however are the same now as then, and will not simply stand by and watch how our allies are treated unjustly and help them only in the future—their suffering is also not in the future. Others have money, ships, stal-

> lions; we have good allies, whom we should not abandon to the Athenians. We also must not respond with tribunals and speeches to harm that is done us not simply in words, but rather help quickly and with all our power. No one can expect us, who have been insulted, to reflect—whoever insults should be the one to reflect at length. Therefore, Spartans, decide for war and the honor of Sparta. Do not let Athens grow even stronger, do not abandon our allies, but go with the Gods against those who have broken the law. (1.86)

These arguments, which make war inevitable, reduce the dispute first to a legal issue and then to a moral one of right and wrong. Practical, strategic questions involving the pursuit of the war are shunted aside—"Others have money, ships, stallions; we have good allies." Temporal questions are dismissed with the declaration that, since the allies are suffering *now*, they must be helped *now*, as quickly as possible, "and not simply in words" but in deeds and with military might. Time is assumed to be on the side of the enemy. Indeed, in a certain sense time *is* the enemy. This is brought out through the comparison Sthenelaïdas makes between the Athenians and the Spartans: Since the Persian wars, he asserts, they, the Athenians, have changed for the worse; by contrast, we, the Spartans, have stayed the same, and thus remain true to ourselves. This fidelity to oneself, defined as resistance to change, makes the decision, in his eyes, ultimately self-evident. The Spartans either will deny themselves by procrastinating, in which he also includes "reflection;" or they will remain true to themselves by deciding to go to war *now*. The future is thus understood as a function of the present, of the *now*, which in turn is understood as a continuation of the past. The Athenians, his argument implies, are powerful, and if the Spartans wait, they will grow even more powerful.

In his compelling analysis of Thucydides, Stahl argues that Thucydides demonstrates again and again how such a notion is disavowed by a "human condition" that subjects all planning to unexpected and uncontrollable outcomes, both because of "external" factors, associated with *tuchē*, and because of self-caused mistakes and misapprehensions. What Stahl does not insist on, but what his interpretation implies, is that these two aspects, internal and external, are profoundly interrelated. Fear, together with desire and lust for power, are dominant factors in provoking such misapprehensions. As we have noted, Sthenelaïdas clinches his argument for going to war immediately through an appeal to the fear of Athens's growing power. Time is not on the side of the Spartans, he suggests. To seize the opportunity is to act now and thus preempt the future, and with it, *tuchē*. A certain kind of targeting defines "opportunity" strictly in terms of the present in order to bring the future, and with it *tuchē*, under control. Such targeting presupposes the prevalence of the present. This in turn involves the effort to transform time and space from media of alteration and alterity to media of self-fulfillment.

What Thucydides' *History of the Peloponnesian War* suggests is that the more one makes such targeting the paradigm of all action, the more that which it denies returns as "the missed opportunity," which is all that remains of chance when its singularity is shunted aside.[12] In short, precisely the insistence that "opportunity" be treated *strictly* as a "target" that can be seized or missed itself misses the mark, because the mark involved is never simply present but always involved with other marks and other opportunities. To take these into account, as we will see, something more and other than target practice is required.

CHAPTER

2

"The Principle of Representation": Carl Schmitt's *Roman Catholicism and Political Form*

> *Chorus.* Citizens of Thebes, behold this Oedipus,
> Who solved famous riddles, a man above all,
> Who cared neither for the frenzy of citizens nor for fortune,
> How he weathered a great fate,
> Therefore, look at what appears at the end of the day,
> Whoever is mortal, and call no one fortunate before
> He has reached life's goal without meeting misery.
>
> —Sophocles, *Oedipus the King*[1]

From the *Odyssey* to the present, a complex and variegated continuity can be found linking the motif and practices of targeting to a certain attitude toward death in what, for want of a better word, I will call the "Western" tradition. In investigating this link, one finds oneself confronted by an *aporia*, which Derrida describes succinctly in his book *Aporias*:

> It is not enough to recall that there are cultures of death and that from one culture to another, at the crossing of borders, death changes face, meaning, language, or even body. . . . One must go further: culture itself, culture in general, is essentially, before anything, even a priori, the culture of death. . . . The very concept of culture may seem to be synonymous with the culture of death, as if the expression "culture of death" were ultimately a pleonasm or a tautology. But only such a redundancy can make legible the cultural difference and the grid of borders. Because

> each culture entails a treatise or treatment of death, each of them treats the end according to a different partition.[2]

"Cultures"—the cultivation of "life"—would thus constitute and differentiate themselves through the distinctive ways they relate to death. At the same time "death" is not something that can be simply "related to" as though it were fixed, stable, and localizable, that is, a straightforward goal or target. This, Derrida observes, is itself inextricably related to death not as a thing but as a word:

> It is well known that if there is one word that remains absolutely unassignable or unassigning with respect to its concept and thingness, it is the word "death." Fundamentally one knows perhaps neither the meaning nor the referent of this word. Less than any other noun, save "God"—and for good reason, since their association here is probably not fortuitous—is it possible to attribute [*ajuster*] to the noun "death," and above all to the expression "my death," a concept or a reality that would constitute the object of an indisputably determining experience."[3]

Derrida's passing remark concerning the affinity of the words *death* and *God*, linked in their indeterminacy, is particularly suggestive. Indeed, his later use of the notion of "autoimmunity" to define "religion" takes on a particular relief in view of this affinity. The noun *God* can be understood as an effort to palliate the disruptive effects of the irreducible or insurmountable indeterminacy of the word *death* as the enabling but inevitably equivocal limit of "life." Similarly, the distinction between "life" in general and "human life" can also be understood as an attempt to reduce the "absolute indeterminacy" of the word *death* by giving it a meaning that would be conceivable, in the sense of "imaginable" or "representable," *vorstellbar*. Insofar, however, as the noun *death* resists or exceeds such efforts to give it a determinate meaning, its subordination to the ostensibly proper noun *God* reflects the effort to "defend" and protect the very possibility of stable self-identity, whether individual or collective. And yet given the inevitable divergence between any univocal determination of the noun *God* and the noun *death*—in particular, as Derrida insists, the syntagma *my death*—it might also become necessary to defend against a defense that would sacrifice the singular "my" to the imperatives of a generalizable "self." This, perhaps, is what informs the notion of "autoimmunity": the dialectical *attempt* of the *self* to negate and thereby transcend its singularity qua "I" or ego. If, however, "death" is inseparable from a certain experience of singularity, such strategies of survival cannot but displace the quandary they seek to surmount: they tend to do away with what they ostensibly seek to save.

Be that as it may, Derrida's remarks on the peculiarly enigmatic semantic status of the word *death* become even more pertinent for the problems we have been discussing if we leave Thomas Dutoit's excellent translation for a moment and consult Derrida's French text. The word Derrida uses to designate the impossibility of *attributing* a referent to the word *death* is, in French, *ajuster.* In addition to its English cognate, "adjust," in the sense of "modifying so as to bring into accord," this word can also mean "to take aim," in the sense of *viser.* A dictionary example is *ajuster une cible, un animal*—to aim at a target, an animal. The linking of the two, target and animal, in the dictionary example—and examples, even and especially in dictionaries, are rarely insignificant—raises the question: What if the impossibility of ever "adjusting" a referent to the word *death* and its extremely disturbing consequences could be palliated, temporarily at least, by turning the tables and "adjusting" death so that it seems to become a function of "targeting"? What if such targeting could *adjust* the absolute indeterminacy of "death"—the word and the thing—by linking it, on the one hand, to the target, and, on the other, to the targeter, who would in the process demonstrate the *power,* and perhaps the *right,* to *take* life if not to give it? Would this render the words *death* and *God* more conceivable and thus more bearable?

Such questions can serve as an introduction to a text in which the link between God and death plays a decisive role, namely, Carl Schmitt's essay *Roman Catholicism and Political Form,* first published in 1923. At the time of its publication,

Schmitt, who was professor of jurisprudence in Bonn, was known primarily through three previous books: *Political Romanticism* (1919), *Dictatorship* (1921), and *Political Theology* (1922). He was already considered to be one of the leading political thinkers of the time and one of the few legal scholars who affirmed the importance of Catholicism to his thought. Nevertheless, Schmitt's relation to Catholicism was never a simple one, either personally or intellectually. Politically he was close to the Catholic Center Party, and the 1923 essay has been read as a theoretical elaboration of this political position. Intellectually, however, his arguments conspicuously shunned both canonical sources of Catholic political thought, such as the natural right theory of Aquinas, and more modern thinkers, such as those associated with the tradition that Schmitt had attacked in *Political Romanticism.* Personally, his relations to the Church were no less ambivalent. In the early twenties, he attempted to dissolve a first marriage, but despite repeated efforts, his request for an annulment was refused. When it became clear that the Church would not grant his request, Schmitt remarried and was immediately excommunicated. This situation lasted from 1926, the year of his second marriage, until 1950, when his second wife died and the excommunication was lifted.

At the time he wrote *Roman Catholicism and Political Form*, to be sure, he had not yet arrived at an open break with the Church. Nevertheless, this text makes clear that Schmitt's approach to Catholicism, particularly in its political dimension, is by no means conventional or orthodox. This is clear from his opening sentence, which, as so often in Schmitt's writing, is both apodictic and theatrical:

> There exists an anti-Roman feeling [*Affekt*]. It provides the struggle against Popism, Jesuitism, and Clericalism, which has agitated European history for centuries, with a gigantic reserve of religious and political energy. Not merely fanatic sectarians, but whole generations of pious Protestants and Greek-Orthodox Christians have seen in Rome the Anti-Christ or the Babylonian Whore of the Apocalypse. This image is more profound and powerful

> in its influence than any economic calculation. Its aftereffects are long-lasting.[4]

This initial observation, which has lost some, but by no means all of its relevance today, is of interest particularly for the way in which it broaches the problem with which Schmitt is concerned in this text: the political dimension of Roman Catholicism. It begins with a characteristically negative determination—"There is an anti-Roman feeling"; *Es gibt einen antirömischen Affekt*—which describes, first, a situation of conflict and, second, a conflict driven by factors that are not simply rational: by "affects," that is, feelings or emotions. Wherein these feelings consist is not yet specified. They are simply stated as a fact: "There is"; *Es gibt.* This is particularly striking, since the fact concerns feelings, which are usually attributed to a subject. This is why it is difficult to find a satisfactorily idiomatic translation of what in German is perfectly idiomatic. In English we tend to think of "feelings" or "emotions" as something someone "has," or at least that pertain to someone. The German word Schmitt uses, by contrast, has a subtly different field of connotations: an "affect" is something that "affects" someone, which implies that it comes from *elsewhere.* What Schmitt is describing, then, is an "affect" by which one is overcome, rather than a feeling or emotion that one "has." An affect, unlike a feeling, can never be understood as the exclusive property of an isolated individual, since its origin lies elsewhere. Yet it is still bound up with individuals, even if it originates elsewhere, which is what distinguishes it from the word used in the English translation of Schmitt's text, namely, *temper.*

This affect is clearly negative: it is "anti-Roman." That would assimilate it to a kind of hatred or, at the very least, mistrust. But, as Schmitt's text soon makes clear, this aggressive aspect of the anti-Roman affect is itself a response to another feeling that is often less conscious: namely, *fear.* In this particular case, it is "fear of the unfathomable [*unfassbaren*] power of Roman Catholicism" (6/14). Roman Catholicism produces anxiety because it is difficult, literally, to "grasp [*fassen*]," to "get a handle on." This anxiety is both epistemic and political.

It is epistemic because it involves the inability to "grasp" or "comprehend"; if something cannot be grasped, it is much harder to control, more unpredictable, and therefore potentially more threatening, at least to a self that seeks to stay the same over time. At the same time, this suggests that the process of cognition, generally held to be affectively neutral, may indeed have a defensive dimension: to comprehend something would be desirable, from this standpoint, insofar as it could be seen to put that thing in its place, thus rendering it locatable and potentially less threatening because more controllable. Precisely this expectation, Schmitt emphasizes, is challenged by the history of Roman Catholicism: "Its elasticity," he acknowledges somewhat ironically, "is in fact astonishing," since throughout its history the Church has demonstrated a remarkable ability "to form alliances with the most opposed tendencies and groups" (6/4).

To describe this disconcerting "elasticity," Schmitt introduces a phrase that, perhaps because it is in Latin, sounds as though it might belong to the doctrinal history of Roman Catholicism. As we shall see, however, nothing could be further from the truth. Nevertheless, this term will function in the essay as a key concept in Schmitt's determination of the political dimension of Roman Catholicism. Its implications, as we shall see, will reach far beyond the limits of this single essay. The term is *complexio oppositorum*. It sounds very similar to another Latin concept that does indeed play an eminent role in the history of Catholic thought, as well as in that of philosophy in general: the notion of *coincidentia oppositorum* developed by Nicolas of Cusa. In Schmitt's essay, however, a *complexio* is quite distinct from a *coincidentia*. As elaborated by Nicolas, the latter term suggests that the opposites converge in the transcendent infinitude of God. Schmitt's notion of *complexio*, by contrast, is resolutely this-worldly and is conceived strictly with respect to the finite world of phenomena. It will therefore provide the foundation of Schmitt's attempt to explain the specifically *political* force of Roman Catholicism, which he will clearly distinguish from its theological and dogmatic dimension.

In fact, despite its ostensibly Latin history, the phrase has little to do with Catholic dogma. It comes originally from alchemy, and in Schmitt's lifetime was employed by the great Protestant historian Adolf von Harnack, who used it to explain, if not justify, the "anti-Roman affect."[5] In Schmitt's essay, by contrast, the phrase serves to explain not only the fear and enmity provoked by the Church but also its unique position in the political realm. The arguments supporting this shift in evaluation emerge as soon as Schmitt begins to elaborate the notion. The history of the Church, he writes:

> displays instances of astounding assimilation [*Anpassung*], but also of rigid intransigence, of the capacity for the most manly resistance and for feminine docility, arrogance and humility strangely mixed. . . . But also theologically the *complexio oppositorum* dominates everywhere. Old and New Testament are equally honored [*gelten nebeneinander*], Marcion's either-or is answered here with a "[this] as well as [that]" [*Sowohl-Als]*. To Jewish monotheism and its absolute transcendence the doctrine of the Trinity adds so many elements of an immanence of God that here as well many mediations are conceivable. (12/7)

This description entails a considerable shift from the account of nineteenth-century Catholic philosophy given only two years earlier in *Political Theology*: "Wherever Catholic philosophy of the nineteenth century expressed itself with respect to topical issues, it expressed in one form or another the conviction that a great alternative that allows no mediation is becoming unavoidable [*sich aufdrängt*]. 'No medium,' says Newman, exists 'between catholicity and atheism.' All such thinkers formulate a great either-or, whose rigorousness is more reminiscent of dictatorship than of an eternal conversation."[6]

The passage quoted from *Roman Catholicism* demonstrates that Schmitt is still convinced that no discursive mediation is possible between Catholicism and atheism (or technocratic-economistic liberalism), but now he also emphasizes that throughout its history the Church itself has often strayed from the radical "either-or" alternative on which nineteenth-century Catholic conservative thinkers insist. Indeed, the distinctive political specificity of the Church, as Schmitt describes it in this book, derives precisely from its ability to avoid such stark alternatives and the particular kind of *decisiveness* that they impose—but not, to be sure, the imperative of deciding. The decision, however, will not be one that resolves conflict in the kind of higher synthesis familiar to Hegelian (Protestant) philosophy:

> Like the opposition of empty form and amorphous matter, the synthesis of such antitheses also remains foreign to the Catholic Church, which is an entity viscerally [*beileibe*] different from that "higher third" (which by the way is always absent) so dear to the German Philosophy of Nature and History. The Church is therefore prone neither to the despair of antitheses nor to the illusion-filled arrogance of their synthesis. (19/11)

This nonsynthetic, nondialectical character of the Catholic *complexio oppositorum* makes it so difficult to identify with a consistent and nonchanging position. It is what, according to Schmitt, provokes anger and anguish, but also, as we shall see in a moment, exercises a certain fascination. Schmitt cites, approvingly and ironically, Byron's characterization of the Church as "hermaphroditic" (8/5), as yet another indication of its ability to combine properties usually held to be mutually exclusive. And yet precisely in its defiance of a certain logic of identity, such "combining of oppositions," Schmitt notes, appeals to "the ultimate social-psychological roots of human motives and representations [*Vorstellungen*]." What enables the Church thus to hold together elements and attitudes that are normally deemed incompatible is a certain *formalism*, upon which Schmitt will place great weight:

> From the standpoint of the political idea of Catholicism, the essence of the Roman Catholic *complexio oppositorum* resides in a *specifically formal superiority over the material of human life,* one that no previous Empire has known. Here a substantial shaping [*Gestaltung*] of historical and social reality has been achieved, one that, despite its formal char-

> acter[remains [anchored] in concrete existence, *full of life* [*lebensvoll*] and yet rational to the highest degree. (14/8, my emphasis)

The "formal superiority" of which Schmitt writes is, in his eyes, to be clearly distinguished from the notion of "empty form" that, in the passage quoted previously was opposed to "amorphous matter." Rather, this formality is the source of a "superiority [*Überlegenheit*]" that Schmitt does not hesitate to link to the power of an imperium. This link suggests the extent to which Roman Catholicism is, for Schmitt, the heir of imperial Rome. And yet this formality also *distinguishes* the Church from its historical predecessor, for by virtue of its "formal superiority over the material of human life" the Church displays a unique capacity to "shape" "historical and social reality." Wherein resides the source of this "superiority," which, by virtue of its formality, can transcend "the material of human life" while remaining anchored "in concrete existence, full of life and rational to the highest degree"? Schmitt, who has already linked this formal superiority to the *complexio oppositorum*, must now demonstrate just *how* that link functions.

His answer is to introduce what he calls "the principle of representation": "The formal peculiarity of Roman Catholicism consists in the strict execution of the principle of representation. Its particularity can be brought out well through its opposition to the economic-technical mode of thought that dominates today" (14/8). Before we discuss the opposition that Schmitt invokes here to elucidate his "principle of representation," a terminological remark is required. Despite its ostensible identity with its English counterpart, the German word here translated as "representation"—*Repräsentation*—has a set of very different connotations. We are here confronted with a textbook case of what Saussure means when he insists that "value," not "meaning," be considered the defining concept of language qua signifying system. It is not without interest that the concept he thereby calls into question is that of "representation." From this standpoint, the distinctive "value" of the German word *Repräsentation* would be determined, not by what it stands for or represents, but rather by that from which it distinguishes itself. In German, there are several words that overlap with the English word *representation*: first, the word *Vorstellung*, which designates either a mental or a theatrical "representation"; second, the words *Vertretung* or *Stellvertretung*, both of which signify "representation" in the sense of a "delegation" or emissary. Here is an excerpt from the Duden dictionary definition of *Repräsentation*:

> Delegation [*Vertretung*] of a state, a public institution, and so on at a social level, and the pomp and circumstance associated with it [*und der damit verbundene Aufwand*]: The limousine, the palace are strictly means of *Repräsentation*.
>
> A style (of life) oriented toward an elevated social status, with a view toward outward effect.[7]

If in a later text Schmitt will explicitly distinguish "representation" from mere "delegation," it is precisely by virtue of the two other meanings associated with the word in German and described in the dictionary entry just quoted. They associate *social prestige* with *ostentation*, two connotations that the English word does not have.[8] To be sure, the connotation of pomp and circumstance is not one that Schmitt explicitly emphasizes in his discussion of the "representation principle"; indeed, he deliberately rejects the tendency, which he attributes to Protestantism, to think of "the formal" in terms of a "schematic externality" defined by opposition to a more authentic "invisible inwardness" of the individual subject. But his critique of this opposition is based on a positive valorization of the phenomenal aspect of representation. The "formality" of the Catholic Church, according to Schmitt, is not abstract, because it is rooted in "concrete existence" and hence "full of life," *lebensvoll*. As we will shortly see, this apparently innocuous term will prove to be anything but merely "formal," for just such *liveliness* will explain how the "formality" of the Catholic Church has been able to achieve the "substantial shaping"—*substantielle Gestaltung*—of history that has made it into a uniquely powerful and global, if not directly imperial, political force.

As is often the case with Schmitt, however, his initial move in elaborating the "representation principle" is to set it in opposition to the "predominant technical-economistic" way of thinking, which, he argues, tends to make the world into "a gigantic dynamo [*eine riesige Dynamomaschine*]" (22/13): a source of energy, but a mechanical one, which, for Schmitt, is the antithesis of vital force. Thus despite his strictures against a certain romanticism, disposed to construe the world in terms of static oppositions, Schmitt himself does not hesitate, throughout his essay, to recur to the traditional polarity of man versus machine, which he also associates with the opposition of life versus death. This is not without consequences for his conception of political power. In a passage that is no less topical today than it was eighty years ago, Schmitt distinguishes the political position of the Church from that of power politics:

> Control of the earth's oil reserves may perhaps prove decisive in the struggle for world domination, but in this struggle the Vicar of Christ on earth will not be a participant. . . . The political power of Catholicism is based neither on economic nor on military might. Independently of them the Church possesses the pathos of authority in its entire purity. The Church too is a "legal person," but in a manner entirely different from that of a corporation. The latter, typical product of an age of production, is a mode of calculation; the Church, by contrast, is a concrete, personal representation of concrete personality [*eine konkrete, persönliche Repräsentation konkreter Persönlichkeit*]. That it is a grandiose exemplification of legalistic spirit and the true heir of Roman jurisprudence has been acknowledged by everyone familiar with it. In its capacity for legal form resides one of its sociological secrets. But it has the power of this form only because it has the power of representation. (31–32 / 18)

The "secret" of the Catholic Church, in particular of its political power, resides not in its material, financial, or military might, nor even in its juridical and formal procedures, but in its power to represent. This is what makes possible its formal and legalistic spirit, but it is not simply identical with it. In this power of representation resides the distinctive superiority of the Church over its imperial Roman predecessor. To elucidate this relationship, which Schmitt asserts but does not further explicate, it is useful to return briefly to an argument developed in *Political Theology.* Having begun with the assertion that the sovereign can be defined as the one "who decides over the state of exception" he then goes on to argue that such a "decision" is rooted in what he calls the "the problem of juridical form [*das Problem der Rechtsform*]." That problem stems from the fact that the generality of a law entails *an applicability to particular cases* that cannot be derived deductively or intrinsically from the law itself. The same is true for any qualitative proposition, which Schmitt in this text associates with the notion of "norm." The practice of law enforcement upon which the functioning of a legal system depends thus requires an *intervention* that must be construed as being *external* to the system itself but at the same time functions as its indispensable condition of possibility. This intervention Schmitt designates as the "decision."[9] Insofar as this decision is never reducible to any qualitative norm, in the sense of the general propositional *content* of a law, it must be construed as essentially a *formal* act:

> Every concrete judicial decision entails a moment of indifference with respect to its content, because a judicial conclusion can never entirely [*bis zum letzten Rest*] be derived from its premises, so that the fact that a decision is necessary remains an independent and determining factor. . . .
>
> The legal interest in the decision . . . is founded in the peculiarity [*Eigenart*] of the normative, and results from the fact that a concrete given must be judged concretely, even though all that is available to serve as a criterion of judgment is a legal principle in its generality. Hence, in each case a transformation obtains [*liegt vor*]. That a legal idea cannot implement itself on its own [*sich selbst umsetzen*] results already from the fact that it says nothing about who is to apply it. In each transformation [*Umformung*]

> there resides an *auctoritatis interpositio*. A distinctive determination concerning the particular individual or concrete agency [*Instanz*] that can claim such authority is not to be gleaned from the mere legal quality of a sentence or proposition.[10]

The essence of the juridical system, insofar as it has to be applied and enforced, therefore, is not itself derivable from the qualitative (propositional) content of the laws themselves, which remains necessarily general in scope. Rather, it has to come from a nondiscursive, nonconceptual, nonnormative, and yet *authoritative* act of "interposition," as Schmitt puts it. "The formal element in a specifically juridical sense," he writes, "lies in an opposition to this substantive quality," which he also designates as "norm." This opposition is radically heterogeneous: "Normatively considered, the decision is born out of nothing [*aus einem Nichts geboren*]." If we take seriously Schmitt's own use of language, then the decision is "born," not in a manner analogous to the emergence of individual life, but only when considered as a repetition of the divine creation of the world.

The "decision" that for Schmitt constitutes both the legal order and its political condition, namely, sovereignty, is thus by its nature a singular act, not derivable from any generality: it is therefore never a *norm*, but rather a *form*. It is, however, a very specific kind of form, not to be confused either with a transcendental form in the Kantian sense, such as time or space, or with a technical-instrumental one: decision is not precision. It is also not to be confused with "aesthetic form," in which, according to Schmitt, a decision—that is, an applicability to an individual case—is not required. Rather, what is specific to the decision required by the juridical order is that it entails the intervention of an authority that must remain resolutely formal, which is to say, *singular,* but also *concrete*. Such *singular concretion*, Schmitt argues, can be found only in a deciding *subject*, whose decision, far from simply instantiating a more general law, enacts and actualizes the *auctoritas interpositio* without which no law can function. Thus, the *subject* emerges as the *decision in action*: "Given the independent significance of the decision, the subject of the decision acquires a significance that is independent of its content. For the reality of juridical life [*des Rechtslebens*], what is decisive is *who* decides. . . . In the opposition of subject and content of the decision, and in the independent significance of the subject, resides the problem of juridical form" (46).

The non-normative decision that for Schmitt constitutes both the legal order and its political condition, that is, sovereignty, requires embodiment and actualization in a subject whose singularity is the necessary correlative of the decision. The decision through which the law is enforced or applied to a singular event has to be "formal," since it proceeds from a divergence of general from particular, of law from case, a divergence that positive law on its own, by virtue of its endemic generality, can never bridge. It is by virtue of the decisive or, rather, decisional intervention of a singular subject that "law" can be endowed with "life," even though from the point of view of normative legality it is a life born out of "nothing," created *ex nihilo*. As we shall see, this model of the *creation of life out of nothing* will assume a subtle but decisive importance in Schmitt's elaboration of the "principle of representation."

This discussion suggests that the question of "political form" that Schmitt raises in connection with Roman Catholicism derives from the constitutive role of subjective intervention in the judicial process. But apart from the fact that such intervention reflects what for Schmitt is the "concrete" dimension of "life"—which for him by definition (i.e., in general) escapes subsumption under general laws—it remains unclear just how any individual subject should acquire the "authority" to make an effective decision, especially when it is clear, as Schmitt himself states explicitly in *Political Theology*, that a decision is never simply constituted by a "declarative" act: "The very idea of decision precludes that there can be any absolutely declaratory decisions."[11] By extension, this would also include the stipulations of a constitution: that is, it would not be sufficient to ascertain what agency of government is constitutionally empowered to declare a state of exception in order to determine real political sovereignty, but rather what agency or office is *actually capable of imposing* such a decision *effectively*.

What, however, makes a decision "effective"? Is it just the suspension of the existing state of positive law, or does it imply other factors as well? With these questions and considerations in mind, we can return to Schmitt's discussion of the unique political authority of Roman Catholicism. It is, we have read, derived not just from its legalistic formalism but from its power to represent. After our review of Schmitt's discussion of form in *Political Theology,* we will not be surprised to discover that the power to represent draws its force not from a pure formalism but rather from a very specific object, or rather subject, of representation. The Church, Schmitt observes, "represents the *civitas humanas*, it presents [*stellt . . . dar*] at every instant the historical connection with Christ's becoming-human and sacrifice on the cross [*Kreuzesopfer*]; it represents Christ himself, in person, God become Man in historical reality. In this representative dimension (*im Repräsentativen*) resides its superiority over an age of economic thinking" (32/19).

If a skeptical critic seeks to disqualify the Church by asserting that it "represents nothing but representation," then Schmitt replies that this is precisely the source of its strength. The paradigm of representation for Schmitt is the representation of Christ on the cross, and this is for him anything but a mere formality. On the contrary, he argues, such representation has alone shown itself to be capable of "shaping history and social reality" in a "substantial" manner, and this by virtue of a *complexio oppositorum* that prefigures redemption. This prefiguration of redemption is represented as a depiction of individual, corporeal suffering unto death, but in view of resurrection. What is thus brought together in this *complexio* is nothing less than human frailty and finitude, on the one hand, and the promise of eternal life, on the other. Such *bringing-together* does not establish a synthesis here and now, or even a mediation between the extremes, but rather exacerbates the opposition of suffering and survival beyond any dialectical resolution. It is only through the ambiguity of the German formulation, Christ's *Kreuzesopfer*—in which the senses of *victimization* and *sacrifice* cross paths in the word *Opfer*—that representation is constituted as the privileged manifestation of the *complexio op-*

positorum. The representation of the passion of the Christ reenacts the triumph over time by making present at every moment—*stellt dar in jedem Augenblick*—the finitude and frailty of man. But through its representability that finitude and frailty reenact the promise of their opposite: resurrection.[12] Sacrificial victimization becomes the model by which a God becomes human so that humans can become divine. This representation of a past renders visible in the present the hope of a future in which frailty and finitude will be overcome. Representation in this sense goes further than visual perception, since what is represented takes on a significance that transcends its visible content: its power resides in its claim to make present, and in so doing, to *make public,* that which otherwise would remain past, absent, and private. By thus appearing to transcend the spatiotemporal and material confines of individual existence, representation can claim to achieve a "substantial shaping" of history. Its substance consists in the community of those who behold and decode the passion of the Christ as the promise of redemption.

The "political idea of Catholicism" thus derives its power and fascination through its ability to give form and shape—that is, to make visible—what in itself can not be reduced to the visible: the hope of the individual that he or she may transcend time, survive, and triumph over death. Such a hope, however, is representable only through its immediate negation, through the depiction of the suffering and passion of Christ on the cross. The promise of self-fulfillment beyond the bounds of mortality is inseparable, not just from suffering and death, but from *deliberately inflicted* suffering and death.[13] The importance of such deliberate infliction emerges when, in a later text, Schmitt makes clear that mere manifestations of death *as such* are incompatible with his notion of representation. In a textbook published four years later, in 1928, entitled *Constitutional Theory* (*Verfassungslehre*), he returns to the question of representation, this time independently of its religious dimension. Nevertheless, he continues to emphasize the privileged relation of representation to the living, which for Schmitt is defined first and foremost through the exclusion of the dead or moribund:

"Something dead [*etwas Totes*], something inferior [*etwas Minderwertiges*] or worthless, something base cannot be represented. Such things lack the higher kind of being that is capable of elevation to the status of public existence. Values such as grandeur, nobility, majesty, fame, dignity, and honor suggest the particularity of such heightened and representable being."[14] Thus, to reproduce "something dead" or "inferior" is not to "represent" in the sense that Schmitt associates with the political idea and power of Catholicism. Why this should be so, his formal analysis of representation in the *Verfassungslehre* makes clear: "To represent means to make an invisible being visible and present it through a publicly present being [*öffentlich anwesendes Sein*]. The dialectic of the concept resides in the fact that the invisible is presupposed as absent and yet at the same time [*gleichzeitig*] is made present. That is not possible with just any kind of being but presupposes a particular kind" (209–10).

Representation thus creates a medium of *public presence* by, in a certain sense, spatializing time through simultaneity and superimposition: that which is absent is "at the same time" made present, placed "there," out in front of beholders, but in close proximity. Time is treated as a medium of assimilation—as "the same time [*gleichzeitig*]—rather than as one of difference, change, alteration. The individual who *stays the same over time* Schmitt designates as a "person." The person persists. This is what distinguishes representation from the dominant technical-economic mode of thought and action, which Schmitt, following Max Weber, sees as essentially a mode of calculation. By contrast, he insists that "The idea of representation, . . . is so dominated by the thought of personal authority that both the representative and the represented must display personal dignity. Representation in the strict sense has to involve a person . . . or an idea, which, as soon as it is represented, personifies itself" (35–36).

How is this notion of "person" compatible with the notion of "representation"? The Church, we recall, represents, according to Schmitt, "Christ himself, in person." But what distinguishes that person is a certain self-sacrifice: in this case,

Christ's *Kreuzesopfer.* And insofar as representation entails the making present of what is and remains absent or, rather, is at the same time both present *and* absent, present *as* absent, the "personal" qualities involved here are not simply those of an empirical individual. The following example, provided in Schmitt's *Constitutional Theory,* suggests a possible answer to this question:

> That *X* steps up in place of an absent *Y*, or for several thousand such *Y*'s, is thus not in itself a representation. A particularly simple historical example of representation obtains when a king is represented to another king through an emissary (i.e., a personal representative, not through an agent, who carries out tasks for him). In the eighteenth century this kind of "representation in an eminent sense" was clearly distinguished from other processes of delegation. (210)

What appears here to distinguish the "personal emissary," who represents the king to another king, from a mere "agent" who carries out tasks is a certain continuity, an ability through a surrogate to be present in more than one place at a time or, rather, to stay the same across time and space. This ability thus suggests the overcoming of finite bodily limitations of bodily individuals, which is why for Schmitt it is not the concept of the biological individual or group that defines the "person" as representative, but rather its ability to be elsewhere and other and yet *at the same time to remain itself.*

The "person," then, is the individual capable, in this very specific sense of *representing itself* and thereby of transcending the limitations of all living individuals. It is on this basis that Schmitt, again in *Constitutional Theory,* can assert that the "idea of representation" is decisive in establishing the identity and unity of a political entity, a "people": "The idea of representation rests on the fact that a people existing as a political unity possesses a higher and more intensive mode of being than does a naturally existing human group that just happens to be living together [*dem natürlichen Dasein einer irgendwie zusammenlebenden*

Menschengruppe]" (210). If the political unity of a "people" depends upon "representation," and representation in turn depends upon a certain transcendence of the "person," then the question to be answered is how such transcendence is achieved. In the exemplary case of Christ, it is the *Kreuzesopfer*, in which dying takes on a sacrificial and redemptive significance. Through such sacrifice, "the natural existence" of human life is overcome, and for Schmitt this overcoming provides a model for the constitution and survival of a political entity. In *The Concept of the Political*, published in 1932, Schmitt will describe that process as a function of the "friend-enemy grouping." Politics, for him, will always involve the exercise of power in a situation of conflict. But is not the "friend-enemy grouping" already anticipated in the *Kreuzesopfer* of Christ as the paradigmatic object of representation, insofar as that *Opfer* is precisely the result of the deliberate acts of *enemies*, which in turn are echoed by the deliberate act of Jesus in accepting and affirming this fate? The other as death-bringing enemy thus emerges, paradoxically if not dialectically, as the enabling condition of a life that sustains itself through self-sacrifice, whether qua individual or qua community.

To be sure, once again, neither in this text nor, to my knowledge, elsewhere does Schmitt dwell on or even mention this aspect of "the passion of the Christ." But through its absence it implicitly frames his notion of representation as the paradoxical overcoming of the opposition of presence and absence, life and death—an overcoming that in turn founds political unity and community—beginning with the *civitas humana* of the Church. Christ does not just die: he is put to death deliberately, and he accepts this death no less deliberately. Through this dual deliberateness, death is defined as the result of human intentions and acts—of sin.

Christ, in short, is *targeted*, and only *as target* can he become the sacrificial model of a process of redemptive representation that seeks to deprive death of the "sting" of its ambiguous irreversibility. Representation can thus present itself as doing away with alterity by appropriating it. Targeting through representation thus emerges, for Schmitt at least, as the condition under which a natural, finite, nondescript *grouping* can resurrect and transform itself into a unified and enduring political community. But without an enemy to change anxiety into fear, fear into guilt, and guilt into aggression, a happy ending to the process would be unthinkable.

All of this remains implicit, unsaid, and indeed barely legible in *Roman Catholicism and Political Form,* since the form of Roman Catholicism only becomes "political" in and through its absence. But its effect and affects—the "anti-Roman affect"—which frame Schmitt's account will have to wait for the publication of *The Concept of the Political* to assume a concrete shape: namely, as the indispensable enemy. With an important difference: with the advent of the "concept" of the political, its "form" will take a back seat, and with it, the "principle of representation." From now on, politics for Schmitt will define itself through the *targeting of the enemy, genitivus objectivus* and *subjectivus*. But the redemptive value of killing will remain the not so public secret of its success.

CHAPTER

3

Wartime: Freud's "Timely Thoughts on War and Death"

The Drive to War

In the years following the Franco-Prussian war and the ensuing unification of Germany, Nietzsche published a series of four essays under the general title *Untimely Observations* (1873–76). In the introduction to the second of these, "The Use and Abuse of History," Nietzsche explains and defends his title: "This observation is also untimely, because what the times [*die Zeit*, the age] are rightly proud of, its historical cultivation [*Bildung*], I try to understand here as damage, breakage, and deficiency, because I believe indeed that we are all suffering from a consuming historical fever and at the very least ought to recognize *that* we are suffering from it."[1] Against the "consuming historical fever" and fervor, Nietzsche felt obliged to remind his countrymen that "a great victory" is also "a great danger," since victory "is more difficult for human nature to support than defeat; indeed, it actually seems easier to achieve such a victory than to prevent it from becoming an even greater defeat" (155).

The danger of seeing victory turn into defeat Nietzsche linked to the "widespread, indeed universal error" into which "public opinion" had fallen: namely, of believing that, together with German military might, "German culture as well had emerged victorious from the battle." This, Nietzsche warned, could lead not just to the "defeat" but to the "extirpation of the German spirit [*Geistes*] in favor of the German *Reich*" (156). It was against this temper of the times—the belief in historical progress as epitomized in the emergence of the German *Reich*—that Nietzsche directed his "untimely observations."

Some forty years later, in 1915, one year after the outbreak of what was already was known as "The Great War," the editors of the psychoanalytical journal *Imago* appealed to Freud for an article, since the war had made it difficult to collect contributions. Freud responded with a text whose title recalled, if only by inversion, Nietzsche: "Timely Thoughts on War and Death."[2] The text consisted in two relatively independent although interrelated essays, the first dealing with the "disenchantment" produced by the war, and the second with changes in the attitude to death. Although Freud called his essays "timely"—*zeitgemäß*—his relation to the "times" was no less critical than had been that of Nietzsche. The difference was simply that the faith in historical *Bildung*, which Nietzsche had questioned, had in the meantime been badly shaken by the destructiveness of the "great war." The temper of the times that Freud began by describing was therefore no longer one of fervor and confidence, but rather one of "disenchantment":

> When I speak of disenchantment, everyone immediately knows what is meant. . . . One told oneself that wars could not stop as long as peoples live under such diverse conditions of existence. . . . One was therefore prepared for the fact that wars between primitive and civilized peoples, between races of different skin color, even wars with and among the less developed, more savage peoples [*Völkerindividuen*] of Europe, would occupy humanity for a long time to come. But one had hoped something else . . . of the great world-ruling nations of the white race . . . whose creations include technical progress in the domination of nature as well as artistic and scientific cultural values—of these peoples one had expected that they would know how to resolve differences and conflicts of interest in some other manner. (325–26)

Thus, although one knew that it was unlikely that European civilization would put an end to war, one still expected that armed conflict would be conducted in conformity with "all the international agreements and institutions" that had been established to limit its destructiveness. These were the hopes and indeed expectation that the Great War revealed to be nothing but an illusion:

> Then the war in which we had refused to believe broke out, and it brought—disenchantment. Not only is it more bloody and more destructive than any previous war, because of the enormously increased perfection of weapons of attack and defense; it is at least as cruel, as embittered, as implacable as any that has preceded it. The war exceeds all the limitations instituted in peacetime and known as international law [*Völkerrecht*]; it ignores the prerogatives of the wounded and of the physician, the distinction between civil and military sections of the population, the claims of private property. It overwhelms with blind rage anything that stands in its way, as though there were to be no future and no peace afterwards. It tears up all bonds of community among the warring peoples and threatens to leave behind an embitterment that will make any renewal of these bonds impossible for many years to come. (328–29)

The unprecedented violence of the "great war" reveals a state of mind that is ready to ignore the longer-term perspective upon which all rules and agreements are based in order to strike its targets more effectively and achieve its immediate goals. This mentality, as Freud puts it, tends to act "as though there were . . . no future and no peace afterwards," but only eternal war. How such actions and the state of mind they reflect should have become possible is the question with which Freud struggles throughout this essay. Needless to say, if anything it has become even more urgent since then. The responses he provides in it are neither simple nor straightforward. One reason for this is that they do not simply survey, as though from a secure distance, the phenomena they address, but rather are drawn into their movement. The result is not merely Freud's description of "disenchantment," but also a sense of confusion that is palpable in the opening lines of the text:

> Caught up [*gepackt*] in the whirlwind [*Wirbel*] of wartime, one-sidedly informed, without distance from the great transformations that have already occurred or that are beginning to, and without a glimmer of the future taking shape, we ourselves lose our bearings [*werden wir selbst irre*] with respect to the significance of impressions that crowd in on us as well as to the values of the judgments we form. (324)

It is revealing to compare this opening with the way Carl Schmitt begins the two essays discussed in the previous chapter, *Roman Catholicism and Political Form* and *Political Theology.* Schmitt, as we have seen, had a strong sense of the importance of what he called "grand rhetoric," without which his "representation principle" could not implement itself.[3] His own writing style provides us with many instances of such "grand rhetoric," and nowhere more than in these two opening lines:

> There exists an anti-Roman affect (*Roman Catholicism*).

> Sovereign is he who decides over the state of exception (*Political Theology*).

Both of these openings consist in short, apodictic assertions relating to conflict situations. Both act out what they simultaneously describe, but in complicated ways. The speaker-writer-author is the "sovereign" source of a "decision" that both embodies and "excepts" itself from what it states. Schmitt's *statement* defining sovereignty takes exception to the "exception" by *deciding* that it is a *state.* And yet the decisiveness of the statement presupposes a vantage point that implies a certain distance from what it is addressing. Such distance, by contrast, no longer obtains in the opening lines of Freud's essay. The experience of being, literally, "seized"—*gepackt*—"caught up" in and by "the whirlwind of wartime" entails precisely the collapse of all distance. The immediate effect is that those who are caught up in the whirlwind lose, not simply their "bearings," but, even more, their capacity to make reliable judgments. A "decision," to be sure, is precisely *not* a *judgment,* and in this sense the "whirlwind" described by Freud does not rule out the kind of sovereignty described by Schmitt. But the fact remains that, whereas Schmitt begins with apodictic assertions, Freud begins with confusion, if not chaos.

Like Schmitt, to be sure, and indeed like any scholar or scientist, Freud does have something he can fall back on, even in times of war. A letter he had written a year earlier, shortly after the outbreak of the war, to a Dutch physician makes this position clear:

> *Respected Colleague,*
> Under the influence of this war I venture to remind you of two assertions psychoanalysis has put forward which have certainly not contributed to its popularity with the public at large. From the dreams and slips of healthy people as well as from the symptoms of neurotics, it has concluded that the primitive, savage and evil impulses of man have not disappeared from any individual, but rather persist, albeit repressed in the unconscious, as we put it in our terminology, and await only an opportunity to become active once again.
>
> Psychoanalysis has taught us further, that our intellect is both weak and dependent, a plaything and tool of the dispositions of our drives and our affects, and that all of us behave either insightfully or obtusely as dictated by our attitudes and inner resistances.
>
> And if you now take a look at what is happening in this time of war: the acts of cruelty and of injustice for which most of the civilized peoples are responsible . . . , you will have to acknowledge that psychoanalysis was not wrong in its two assertions.[4]

The psychoanalytic theory of the drives may provide an explanation for the violence of the war—but as we shall see, even for Freud that explanation is not sufficient. Nevertheless, it is the best he has to offer, at least in this first part of the essay. To be sure, any attempt to account for a phenomenon such as war in terms of a theory of "drives," developed through the interpretation of the behavior of individuals, runs the risk of being dismissed as reductively psychologistic. Freud seems to provoke just such a rebuke when he repeatedly uses the term, *Völkerindividuen*—literally, "people-" or "nation-individuals"—to describe supra-individual, political entities. Yet such a reproach misconstrues the specific character of the Freudian theory of drives, which has little to do with traditional "psychology." Rather, the theory of drives recalls the observation of Novalis in his *Encyclopedia* that "the genuine dividual [*Dividuum*] is also the genuine individual" (§1363). The drive *divides* the psyche and body it occupies and establishes a *relation of forces* that is by no means "in-dividual" in the sense of indivisible, but rather eminently divisible. It divisions are then subject to constant negotiation and struggle.

Moreover, the divisive thrusts and counter-thrusts, replacements and displacements that constitute the intricate dynamics of the drive as Freud describes it involve a highly complex relation to what could be called its *target*; the latter is split between its "goal" or "aim" (in Freud's German, its *Ziel*), and its "object," through which that aim manifests and localizes itself. In an essay published the same year as his "Timely Thoughts," Freud describes the drive in the following terms:

> The "drive" [appears] as a borderline concept between the psychic and the somatic, as psychic representative [*psychischer Repräsentant*] of the stimuli stemming from within the body and reaching the psyche. . . . The character of impulsion is a general property of the drives, indeed its essence. Each drive is a bit of activity. . . . The *goal* [*Ziel*] of a drive is always the satisfaction that can be attained only through the surmounting of the stimulation at the source of the drive. However, even though this final goal [*Endziel*] remains unchanged for each drive, different ways can lead to the same final goal, so that for any one drive many different proximate or intermediate goals can emerge, which can be combined with one another or exchanged for each other. . . . The *object* of the drive is that in which or through which the drive can reach its goal. It is the most variable aspect of the drive, is not originally

> linked to it but only attributed to it by virtue of its capacity to make satisfaction possible. It is not necessarily a foreign object but can just as well be a part of one's own body. In the course of the drive's life [*Lebensschicksale*] there is no limit to how often it can be changed; this displacement of the drive can play the most significant roles.[5]

What distinguishes the dynamics of the drive from other goal-directed behavior is the divergence between its "goal" or *Ziel*, and its *object*. The *aim* or goal of a drive never changes: it is the reduction of an existing state of tension, which Freud designates as "satisfaction." Its *object*, by contrast, is extremely variable, since it bears no intrinsic relation to the drive. Rather, it consists in whatever is associated with a reduction of tension. In other words, the heterogeneity of *goal* and *target* qua *object* constitutes the specificity of what Freud calls "drive," *Trieb*. At the same time, however volatile the relation of drive and object may be, every drive must nevertheless be linked to an object in order to attain its goal: "satisfaction"—a quantitative and differential reduction of tension—necessarily passes by way of an object, although it is never an intrinsic quality of the object as such.

This necessary but volatile relationship of drive to object explains the rather unusual term used by Freud to designate the way in which psychic energy relates to mental representations. That term is *Besetzung,* which in German signifies "occupation," also (but not exclusively) in the military sense. It can also signify a theatrical "cast." What the two have in common is that the place "occupied" is "not originally linked to" its occupiers (whether military or theatrical), any more than the object is to the drive that "occupies" it. The "drive" thus defines itself by "occupying" an object and/or its representation, which serve it as a means toward attaining its ultimate aim, a reduction in tension. And yet it is precisely the link between these two essentially heterogeneous spheres—that of the aim or goal, and that of the object—that constitutes the "drive."

The word Freud uses to designate this intermediary status of the drive, *Repräsentant*, "representative," assumes a strange resonance in the aftermath of the preceding chapter. The word functions in a way that is both similar to and yet different from Schmitt's "representation principle." It is similar insofar as the drive, through its representative function, makes visible what nevertheless is essentially invisible: "stimuli stemming from the interior of the body." Needless to say, these invisible stimuli are quite different from the Creator-God-Father who is incarnated in the "person" of Christ. Here, what the drive "represents" is a certain *transition* from the somatic to the psychic. But it is not a transfiguration of one into the other. The process of representation thus remains discontinuous and heterogeneous. What is represented, in part via the "occupied object," remains radically non-objective, since it consists in a differential relation of forces: "stimuli" contributing to a tension that the drive strives to reduce.

The difference that separates Schmitt's "representation principle" from Freud's "psychic representative" can be measured in the concepts associated with each. For Schmitt, as we have seen, the *complexio oppositorum* marks the conjoining of opposites to produce a certain order and unity, although one that continues to depend on the structure of opposition—the "enemy" or "state of exception"—in order to maintain itself. For Freud, the heterogeneous representation of the drive calls into question precisely such unity:

> These primitive impulses undergo a lengthy process of development before they are allowed to become active in the adult. They are inhibited, directed towards other aims and fields, become commingled, change their objects, turn in part against one's own person [*gegen die eigene Person*]. Reaction-formations against certain drives assume the deceptive form of a change in their content, as though egoism had changed into altruism, or cruelty into pity. These reaction-formations are facilitated by the circumstance that some drive impulses appear almost from the first in pairs of opposites—a very remarkable state of affairs that is foreign to the popular mind [*populären Kenntnis*] and that has been called "*ambivalence of feeling.*" The most

> easily observed and comprehensible instance of this is the fact that intense love and intense hatred are so often to be found together in the same object. Psychoanalysis adds to this that the two opposed feelings not infrequently also have the same person as object. (281, my emphasis)

Freud's notion of *ambivalence* is characteristically linked to the turning of the drives back "against one's own person," a reflexive movement that, far from producing unity, dislocates it. Whether the person "itself" or the drive "itself," it is the "self" that is split through the "ambivalence of feeling": what is "felt" is incompatible with what or who is "feeling." The representation of the drives, as Freud construes it, does not establish the transcendent unity of the *person*, as in Schmitt's notion, but rather disarticulates it.

Thus, if Schmitt is fond of quoting Clausewitz's famous dictum that "war is nothing but the continuation of political intercourse with a mixture of other means,"[6] one could say that, for Freud, war can be considered to be the continuation of the "destiny" of the drive, which consists in a struggle to "occupy" and control targets that it is nevertheless ready to forsake and replace at any moment. The "destiny" of the drive thus knows neither lasting victory nor enduring peace; but only ongoing struggle marked by an occasional truce.

This is why Freud, after having begun his "Timely Thoughts" by noting the widespread "disenchantment" (287) and turmoil caused by the war, winds up the first section of his essay by suggesting that such responses were the result of an illusion: "Our disappointment and painful disenchantment . . . were based on an illusion that held us prisoner. In reality [the human collective-individuals: peoples and states] have not sunk as low as we feared for the simple reason that they had not climbed as high as we thought" (336). Insofar as human activity is determined by "drives," it is no wonder that it does not follow the teleological pattern generally attributed to historical development, at least in the nineteenth and much of the twentieth century:

> Psychic developments possess a peculiarity that can be found in no other developmental process. When a village

> grows up into a city, a child into a man, the village and child disappear into the city and into the man. Memory alone can inscribe the old traits into the new image; in reality, the old materials or forms have been done away with and replaced by the new ones. A psychic development proceeds differently. This incomparable state of affairs can be described only by asserting that each earlier level of development remains preserved next to the later ones that emerged out of it. Succession here involves coexistence, although the entire sequence of transformations has, after all, operated upon the same materials. . . . The primitive psychic state is in the fullest sense imperishable [*unvergänglich*]. (337)

This replacement of succession by simultaneity is reflected in Freud's propensity to speak of the movement of the drive in terms of "destiny"—*Schicksal*—rather than of "development," much less "history." The dynamic of the drive in its twists and turns does not "unfold" an internal essence, but follows a pattern imposed upon it by the specific heterogeneity of its representative function.

And yet, having elaborated the close connection between the psychoanalytic theory of "drives" and the "disenchantment" and turmoil produced by the excessive violence of the war, Freud still has to acknowledge that the decisive question remains unanswered:

> We had hoped, certainly, that the grandiose community of interests brought about through commerce and production would produce the beginnings of such a compulsion [to morality]; but it seems that nations [*Völker*] obey their passions far more readily these days than their interests. At best, they make use of their interests in order to *rationalize* their passions; they put forward their interests in order to justify satisfying their passions. Why nation-individuals [*Völkerindividuen*] in fact despise, hate, and detest each other, even in peacetime, each nation the others, remains, it is true, a mystery. I cannot say why [*Ich weiß es nicht zu sagen*]. In this case it is as though all the moral

> achievements of individuals are obliterated once a multiplicity [*eine Mehrheit*] or indeed millions come together, and only the most primitive, most ancient, and crudest attitudes survive. (340)

It is no doubt in order to find a more suitable answer to this unanswered question posed by the war that Freud sees himself constrained, in the second part of his essay, to address "Our Relation to Death."

Killing the Mandarin

Freud concludes this second section, and with it the essay as a whole, by suggesting that "the old saying, *si vis pacem, para bellum*; if you want to preserve peace, arm for war" requires an update. "It would be timely to change it: *si vis vitam, para mortem*; if you want to endure life, prepare yourself for death" (355). This provides the text with what is at best an ironic conclusion, since everything that has been discussed in it serves only to demonstrate just how difficult it is to follow such advice. However, Freud's point of departure is to show how far modern culture and society are from even acknowledging that such a task might be necessary:

> We showed an unmistakable tendency to push death aside, to eliminate it from life. We tried to silence it to death [*ihn totzuschweigen*]; we even have a saying [in German]: to think of something as though it were death [i.e., to think something unlikely or incredible]. As though it were our own death, naturally. One's own death is of course unimaginable [*unvorstellbar*: unrepresentable], and whenever we make the effort to do so, we can ascertain how we actually continue to remain present as spectators [*daß wir eigentlich als Zuschauer weiter dabei bleiben*]. Hence the psychoanalytic school could venture the assertion that at bottom no one believes in his own death or, what amounts to the same, that *in the unconscious each of us is convinced of his own immortality.* (341; my emphasis)

"In the unconscious each of us is convinced of his own immortality"—just how is this assertion to be understood? The remainder of Freud's essay can productively be read as an attempt to provide an answer to this question, although it is a question that Freud never explicitly asks.

To think of one's own death as one normally thinks of other things, namely, by representing it, is to transform it into a spectacle and ourselves into spectators and thereby to miss what distinguishes it from all other worldly events and phenomena: the cessation of our being in the world. To represent one's own death is thus necessarily to misrepresent it. At best, one can imagine it only as the death of another. In peacetime, there is a tendency to avoid even that. But a life out of which death has been banished or marginalized, Freud argues, "loses its interest . . . and becomes as shallow as an American flirt," as distinguished from "a continental love-relationship, the serious consequences of which must constantly be kept in mind by both partners" (343). And yet, how can one—"continental" or not—"keep in mind" a "consequence" that remains strictly unimaginable? One possible if problematic response is to be found, Freud observes, in "the world of fiction, literature, theater":

> There we still find people who know how to die—*who, indeed, even manage to kill someone else.* Only there can the condition be fulfilled that makes it possible for us to reconcile ourselves with death: namely, that behind all the vicissitudes of life we should still be able to *preserve a life intact. . . . In the realm of fiction we find the plurality of life that we need. We die with the hero with whom we have identified ourselves; yet we survive him*, and are ready to die again just as safely with another hero.
>
> It is evident that war is bound to sweep away this conventional treatment of death. Death can no longer be denied; we are compelled to believe in it. People really die, and no longer one by one, but many, often tens of thousands, in a single day. And death is no longer a chance event. (343–44; my emphasis)

In "fiction" people find "the plurality of life that we need"—need, in order to be able to represent it and yet still survive. Not the "plurality of lives" but the "plurality of *life*," which is thus reformulated to eliminate the finitude that is the fate of all living beings insofar as they are singular and that prevents one from representing one's "own" death. In fiction, literature, and theater, this dilemma is ostensibly surmounted—but only under the condition that death is displayed as something that affects others alone. In this context it is significant that Freud links a certain *know-how* concerning *how to die* with the ability "to kill someone else." This indicates the ambivalent and ambiguous relation of war to death. On the one hand, "Death can no longer be denied; we are compelled to believe in it. People really die, and no longer one by one, but many . . . death is no longer a chance event" (344).[7] If in wartime death can no longer be regarded as an accident, however, it can still be considered something that happens essentially to others. In this respect, Freud notes that war divides society into two very different groups: those who are directly involved in combat and thus exposed to its risks, and those who are not. For the latter group, among whom Freud counts himself, the reality of the war is not generally accessible through direct sensory perception (assuming something of the sort exists, *concesso non dato*), but largely through the intermediary of the media. And to the extent to which these media are able to present war as an essentially fictional spectacle, as an ongoing narrative—something to be seen and survived—it can sustain the equivocal attitude toward death that Freud retraces to what he calls "prehistoric man [*Urmensch*]":

> Primitive man had a remarkable attitude toward death. Not at all unified, but rather quite contradictory. On the one hand, he took death seriously, recognized it as the abolition of life and used it in this sense; on the other hand, he also denied death and denied it all value. This contradiction was made possible through the fact that he assumed a radically different attitude toward the death of the other, the stranger, the enemy, than toward his own.

> The death of the other was entirely acceptable to him [*war ihm Recht*]. . . . He murdered readily and without scruple.
>
> The prehistory of mankind is thus filled with murder. Even today what our children learn in school as world history is in essence a series of genocides. (345)

Although Freud himself no doubt was convinced of the empirical validity of such speculations, their value is primarily heuristic: they provide a "representation" of the unrepresentable tendencies of the "drives." It is not that "prehistoric man" lives on to determine the course of world history, but rather than the drives are structured in such a way as to reveal the dominant conception of historical progress to be the most powerful "construction" and dissimulation. From this vantage point, belief in the world-historical progress of civilization would be an acting-out of Christian soteriology in which "love of neighbor" takes the form of loving one's neighbors to death: for the death of the neighbor, as other, particularly when it is deliberately inflicted, can be experienced as the demonstration of one's own ability to survive. The not-so-secret content of world history as a teleology of self-fulfillment would thus consist in *the targeting of the other as "mortal" enemy*. At the same time, such targeting, although tenacious and durable, would not remove the doubts that already plagued, in Freud's account, "prehistoric man":

> His own death was certainly just as unimaginable and unreal for prehistoric man as it is for any one of us today. But there was for him one case in which the two opposite attitudes towards death collided and came into conflict with each other; and this case became highly important and productive of far-reaching consequences. It occurred when primeval man saw someone who belonged to him die—his wife, his child, his friend—whom he undoubtedly loved. . . . Then, in his pain, he was forced to learn that one can die, too, oneself, and his whole being revolted against the admission. . . . Yet deaths such as these pleased him as well, since in each of the loved persons there was also something of the stranger. The law of ambivalence of feeling, which to this day governs our emo-

> tional relations with those whom we love most, certainly had a very much wider validity in primeval times. Thus these beloved dead had also been enemies and strangers who had aroused in him some degree of hostile feeling. (346)

Ambivalence marks our relation to death: we mourn the deaths of loved ones, which we experience as a loss and which thus remind us of the possible and indeed inevitable loss of our world. But we also—and here Freud is free of all moralizing—are ready to take solace in a disappearance that can be viewed, however illogically, as confirming the persistence and indeed immortality of those who survive.

Thus, we mourn the death of loved ones and yet in so doing also confirm our survival. We are in their debt and yet as survivors also deny our indebtedness. This acknowledgment of indebtedness to the other, mixed with its denial, is perhaps what links the sentiment of "guilt" to death. "The fear of death," Freud remarks, "which dominates us more often than we know, is . . . usually the outcome of a sense of guilt." But what if the "sense of guilt" were in turn a way of not acknowledging the "fear of death"? And would not such an acknowledgment be rendered all the more difficult to the extent that the linkage of "fear" to "my death" cannot avail itself of the usual means by which such "links" are established, namely, representation? Would not this quandary find at least a temporary "solution" in the displacement of the object of such fear from *my* world—the "homeland"—to the world of the other?

Such a conjecture can perhaps render more comprehensible the function, fascination, and seductive appeal of wartime, as well as its enabling limit. Its major function would be to institutionalize the other as enemy, to legitimize killing, and thus to create an image of death that, precisely qua image, holds it at bay. Far from being unrepresentable, death, as death of the enemy, could become the goal of a deliberate act of targeting, performed by one subject upon another. Death would thus be understood as the result of a conscious decision, which is neither inevitable nor incalculable. Death would thus be redefined as a function of *power*: that over life and death. It would become a means of establishing control and acquiring power over others.

War confirms this perspective, this "relation to death," by allowing it to be made into a spectacle to be observed, or not, by spectators "on the home front." In this respect, there is a profound complicity between "the world of fiction," to which Freud refers, and the world of war: both tend to present death as a spectator sport.

From this point of view, the advent of the electronic media, and in particular of television, appears to have given this age-old sport a new lease on life and a new twist. Once again, Freud provides a scheme through which such twists and turns can be approached:

> It was beside the dead body of someone he loved that [primitive man] invented spirits, and his sense of guilt at the satisfaction mingled with his sorrow turned these newborn spirits into evil demons that had to be dreaded. The [physical] changes brought about by death suggested to him the division of the individual into a body and a soul—originally several souls. In this way his train of thought ran parallel to the process of disintegration that sets in with death. His persisting memory of the dead became the basis for assuming other forms of existence and gave him the conception of a life continuing after apparent death. (347–48)

We are close here to the spectral logic, the "hauntology" elaborated by Derrida in *Specters of Marx*.[8] A certain experience of the body—of the disintegrating body—gives rise, according to Freud, to the spiritualization and idealization that impose the notion of a division of body and soul and thus a possibility of representing the unrepresentable. The disintegrating body gives rise to the idea of the soul, and with it to a "persisting memory of the dead" that in turn suggests "other forms of existence" and ultimately the "conception of a life continuing after . . . death."

This ghostly, spectral life—or at least one aspect of it—is precisely what the electronic media contribute to the institutionalization of death as spectator sport. If technology in general has always been defined as a kind of prosthesis, a substitute for the finitude and deficiencies of the body, commercial broadcast television, vending viewers, as virtual consumers, to advertisers for profit, carries this relation to a qualitatively new stage. Television suspends the exclusive attachment of visual and auditory perception—the power to see and to hear—to individual bodily organs, which is to say, to living, mortal beings located in a particular place at a particular time. With television, such localization, together with the finitude and vulnerability it entails, is ostensibly transcended: with "live" broadcasting, television can claim to be there and here at one and the same time, or almost.

But if television seems to separate the power of seeing and hearing from its traditional linkage to the individual, localized body, the relationship is by no means entirely dissolved but only displaced: from the place of perception to that of reception—or, rather, from a notion of *perception* as self-contained and immediate to a conception of perception as *reception* and response. Today, the television viewer on the "receiving end" is perhaps more isolated, dependent, and vulnerable than before, while at the same time occupying a space in which the representation of lethal violence is entirely compatible with the denial of death. Such denial, like all denial, is anything but stable and self-identical:

> Denial [*Verneinung*] is a way of acknowledging [*zur Kenntnis zu nehmen*] the repressed, indeed, it is actually even a surmounting of repression, but certainly not an assumption or acceptance [*Annahme*] of the repressed. We see here how the intellectual function separates from the affective process. With the help of denial, only a single consequence of the process of repression is undone: that of keeping its representational contents from reaching consciousness. What results is a kind of intellectual acceptance of the repressed while at the same time what is essential in repression is retained [*bei Fortbestand des Wesentlichen an der Verdrängung*].[9]

The denial of death thus goes hand in hand with its "isolation," which is to say, with its association with isolated figures and events. What is dangerous to consciousness and what therefore must be kept from it is not a particular *Vorstellungsinhalt* as such, but the implications that cannot be "contained within" the content (*Inhalt*) of such a representation. What is dangerous, and sometimes even terrifying, in other words, is the *network* of associations it can spawn.[10]

This is why the paradigmatic instance of the defense mechanisms of the ego is not repression, as is commonly assumed—often by Freud himself—but rather what he describes as *isolating*. In isolating—which resembles, Freud notes, the common activity of concentrating, and which therefore is so difficult to separate from the processes of "normal thought"—"an event or idea is not repressed, but rather separated from its affect and from its associative relation . . . so that it stands as though isolated."[11] What is separated in this way involves above all "things that once belonged together," albeit in an ambivalent relationship, and that, because they could not be unified, have therefore "been torn apart in the course of [one's] development." What most belongs together, however ambivalently, and has been torn apart is the *inseparability of self and other*; such sundering first opens the space in which (the semblance of) a clear-cut opposition between self and other can be deployed. One of the privileged forms in which this opposition has emerged, at least in what can be called the "Western" tradition, is the *image*—or, more precisely, the image of objects that are self-contained, *Gestalten*.

By not being representable, containable, or comprehensible in or as such a self-contained image, the relation to my death poses a powerful challenge to the psychic agency constructed on the basis of such images: the ego. One of the indices of this challenge is anxiety, which Freud defines as an "affective signal" insofar as it *signifies* but does not *represent* a danger to the ego. Anxiety is thus the mode of articulation in which the ego experiences its nonrepresentable relation to death.

The efficacy of the broadcast media in times of war as well as of peace derives from their ability both to exploit and to deny—to exploit by denying—such anxiety. The ostensible separability of image from context, of vision and audition from the organs of an individual body, of perception from reception—all this is intensified and also undermined by the media in general, and by television in particular. Such ostentatious separability contributes to the *isolation* of the images and sounds it purveys and to the illusion that they are as self-contained as their spectator-audience. At the same time, the dependency of the broadcast "network" upon relations that cannot be contained or comprehended within isolated sound-images or actors also becomes more manifest. The two extremes of the chain consist, first, in the *network*, which tends to elude direct perception, and, second, in the ostensibly isolated elements that constitute the home theater of reception: the television *set,* sitting in *front* of the viewer, and the surround-speakers all around, as tangibly localized and self-contained as the network is elusively ubiquitous and open to occult forces that escape its control.

Against the "backdrop" of this normal and constitutive ambivalence of the media—whether of the commercial broadcast medium, television, or of the Freudian drive—the whirlwind of wartime can for a while be contained within the reassuring framework of familiar images that make up chapters in an ongoing narrative. The "events" reported on television are presented as episodes in a work in progress, a reality show in serial format, often involving catastrophic violence, anticipated and yet unpredictable, a situation in which teleological thinking finds temporary refuge and in which the viewer can, once again, have the illusion of taking it all in—and surviving. Targeting the enemy as a self-contained objective to be subdued or destroyed also creates a sense of common purpose and cohesion that, temporarily at least, can mitigate the isolation of the viewer by rendering the enemy more "imaginable" and hence more manageable. Such targeting requires an ever more aggressive commitment, however, in order to maintain the isolation, the guilt that arises when indebtedness to the other is denied. The result is a dangerous and destructive spiral of guilt, fear, and aggression that ultimately tends to turn the targeting "inward" against oneself: the "enemy" is no longer simply "out there" but is now feared to have infiltrated the innermost reaches of domesticity.

The consequences of a spiral that Derrida has aptly compared to a process of "auto-immunity"[12] becomes even more evident where the spectacle of war is increasingly dominated, not by traditional enemies, identified with regular and recognizable military units of nation-states, but rather by nonstate, nonregular "terrorists," who act in the shadows. As its name indicates, "terrorism" defines itself through its emotional effects, of which a certain *absence of images* is one of the enabling conditions. Victory can thus be defined as the ability to capture and manipulate these absent images, as with the famous "pack of cards" designating the Iraqi enemies following the occupation of that country in 2003. In the age of the televisual reporting of wars, the absence of images that characterizes "international terrorism" is by no means incompatible with the isolation of imagery that characterizes the reporting of "news" by capitalist media. There is a not so secret resemblance between the terrorist network and the media network: both draw their power from the invisible relationships in which they are enmeshed and which they, for different reasons, seek to dissimulate.

Toward the end of his essay, Freud recounts an anecdote that in many ways sums up much of his previous argumentation:

> In *Père Goriot* Balzac alludes to a passage in the work of J. J. Rousseau, in which this author asks the reader what he would do if—without leaving Paris and naturally without being discovered—he could, through a mere act of will, kill an old Mandarin in Peking, whose death would bring him great benefit. He leaves little doubt that in his mind the life of this dignitary would not be very secure. "*Tuer son mandarin*" has since become proverbial for this secret readiness of modern man. (352)

It is interesting that the proverb Freud chooses to express the murderous propensity of modern man is cited in French, and that the twin sites of the murder are Paris and Peking (and not Berlin or Vienna). What is perhaps even more significant is that the story describes a situation in which individuals are involved in an act of global targeting: the Mandarin in Peking is targeted by the murderer in Paris, and the act to be performed is one that involves nothing more or less than an "act of will." Finally, the "great benefit" that motivates this act can be measured only by *taking the life of another.* Private appropriation involves the privation of life.

That the cost of such privation of the other must also be borne by those who would profit from it is a lesson to be learned from another text of Freud's, to which we will turn in the following chapter.

CHAPTER

4

Doing Away with Freud's *Man Moses*

> What draws the reader to the novel is the hope of warming his freezing life on the death about which he reads.
>
> —W. Benjamin, "The Storyteller"

> La mort ne se laisse pas virtualiser.
>
> —J. Derrida, in a discussion with Jean Baudrillard, *Le Monde*, February 23, 2003

The Way of the Traces

In the summer of 2000, Jacques Derrida gave a keynote address to an international congress of psychoanalysts meeting in Paris. The title of his talk was "Etats d'âme de la psychanalyse," which in the meanwhile has been translated and published in English as "Psychoanalysis Searches the States of Its Soul."[1] Derrida began his talk by asking a series of questions concerning the relation of psychoanalysis to cruelty:

> Let us merely ask ourselves whether, yes or no, what is called "psychoanalysis" does not open up the only way that could allow us, if not to know, if not to think even, at least to interrogate what might by meant by this strange and familiar word *cruelty*, the worst cruelty, suffering *just to* suffer, the making-suffer, the making- or letting-oneself suffer *just for*, if one can still say that, the pleasure of suffering.[2] (239)

To these questions Derrida responded with a provocative assertion about the distinctive quality of psychoanalysis: "No other cognitive discourse stands ready to take an interest in something like cruelty—except what is called psychoanalysis" (240). But if this "cognitive . . . interest" in cruelty for its own sake or, rather, in the "pleasure" that can be produced both by suffering and by making-suffer were to define the distinctive specificity of psychoanalysis, it would also, Derrida suggested, render "its name . . . in turn more undecipherable than ever," perhaps even calling for a "revolution" within psychoanalysis itself. In short, if the question of "cruelty" can be said to define a certain horizon of psychoanalysis, there is no guarantee that this horizon is contained within the parameters of what traditionally has been understood to be its privileged domain, the individual psyche: an extended horizon could bring into play concepts and practices usually reserved for other disciplines—political theory, for instance. This would be so if the linking of suffering and pleasure were to presuppose, as Derrida asserts:

> a certain onto-theological metaphysics of *sovereignty* (autonomy and omnipotence of the subject—individual or state—freedom, egological will, conscious intentionality, or, if you prefer, the ego, the ego ideal, and the superego). The first gesture of psychoanalysis will have been to explain this sovereignty, to give an account of its ineluctability while aiming to deconstruct its genealogy—*which passes also by way of cruel murder.* (244, my emphasis)

The text of Freud that more than any other weaves the different strands mentioned by Derrida into a complex tapestry or network of interrelations is known in English as *Moses and Monotheism.* Written over a period of years beginning in 1936, it was first published in its entirety in 1939, one year before Freud's death. Probably more than any other of his writings, this essay is caught up in the political history of the time, marked by the rise of Nazism and Fascism and the consequent intensification of anti-Semitism throughout Europe. Freud's hope that the Catholic Church might somehow protect Austria from Nazi domination led to his deferring complete publication of the essay until the *Anschluß* (1938) and his ensuing emigration to England. Freud discusses the complex history of the text in the two prefaces to the third and final part of the book, remarking how he had decided to withhold publication pending political developments, and then, once having decided to complete it, how he was compelled to acknowledge that the essay remained profoundly marked by the conditions in which it had been written. One unhappy result, Freud notes, is a tendency to repetition that is never entirely brought under control and about which he, as author, feels quite uneasy. On several occasions, not just in the prefaces to the final section but in the body of the text as well, Freud observes that what he is about to write merely repeats what has already been said elsewhere, not just in previous writings but in this essay itself. It is as if the nonlinear, discontinuous, repetitive temporality that marks the historical process as Freud construes it had contaminated the structure of his text. This is how Freud himself describes the situation:

> The following [final] part of this essay cannot be sent forth into the world without lengthy explanations and apologies. For it is nothing but a faithful, often literal repetition of the first part. . . . I know that this way of presenting my subject is as ineffectual as it is inartistic. I myself disapprove of it wholeheartedly. Why have I not avoided it? The answer is easy for me to find, but rather hard to admit. I have not been able to efface the traces of the unusual way in which this book came to be written.[3]

In making this admission, Freud once again repeats what he had already described earlier in the essay with respect to texts in general, and to the biblical accounts of Moses in particular. These accounts had, according to a scholarly hypothesis that Freud eagerly endorses, sought to expunge all evidence of what Freud takes to be their central and traumatic event: the murder of Moses by the people he had adopted and unified.

About this attempted erasure, Freud notes, in a phrase that was to become one of his most famous: "The distortion of a text is not unlike a murder. The difficulty lies not in executing the deed, but in doing away with its traces" (52/144). In this celebrated formulation, the problem with which Freud will struggle throughout this essay, and elsewhere, is condensed yet also obscured in the ostensibly harmless English phrase "do away with." Everything depends, of course, on just what this entails: What does it mean to "do away with" the "traces" of a murder? To hide them? To expunge them? There is, of course, a difference: to hide something is not to destroy it. In this context, it is significant that one of the earliest uses of this expression documented by the OED emphasizes that "away" initially signified "a way," not just destruction or disappearance. What is "done away with" does not simply cease to exist but rather continues to make its way, even—or especially—if it is removed from view. In this sense, *a way* can *stay with* those who seek to *do away with* it. The German expression used by Freud that is translated as "doing away with" seems to point in the direction of this strange *way*: it is the verb *beseitigen*, literally, to shunt aside or to sideline something. The definition of this verb given in a present-day German dictionary (*Wahrig's Deutsches Wörterbuch*) demonstrates the equivocation: *beseitigen* is defined as "cause to disappear [*zum Verschwinden bringen*]," but also as *aus der Welt schaffen*, roughly translated, "remove from the world,"[4] with the connotation of putting a definitive end to whatever is to be excluded. However, causing something to "leave the world" does not necessarily eliminate the effects it can produce: it merely renders their origin invisible. "Side" (*Seite)*—root of German *beseitigen*—thus seems to frame a field of perception or of consciousness, or perhaps even a horizon (of the living, or the world), but it by no means necessarily signifies a definitive dismissal. Precisely the impossibility of such a dismissal, in its various aspects, will concern Freud in this essay.

Those aspects will include not just the thematic content of his study but the very process of its composition. Freud's striking comparison could be read as suggesting that something akin to a murder stands at the origin not just of the Biblical account of Moses but of his own text as well. The matter is made even more complicated by the series of avowals and disavowals that introduce its final section, in which Freud admits to having withheld and concealed much of his text for the political reasons already mentioned. The result, Freud notes in the preface to the last and final section, is a certain estrangement of author from work:

> The exceptionally great difficulties that have weighed on me during the composition of this essay dealing with Moses—inner misgivings as well as external hindrances—are the reason why this third and final part comes to have two different prefaces, which contradict—indeed, even cancel—each other. . . . Now as then I am uneasy when confronted with my own work; I miss the consciousness of unity and intimacy that should exist between author and work. . . . To my critical faculties this treatise, proceeding from a study of the man Moses, seems like a dancer [*wie eine Tänzerin*], balancing on one toe. Had I not been able to find support in the analytic interpretation of the exposure myth and pass thence to Sellin's suggestion concerning Moses' end, the whole treatise would have [had] to remain unwritten. (69–71/159–60)

Although it does not appear in the published English translation I have just cited, Freud compares the precarious balancing act his text is compelled to exercise not just to a "dancer" but to a *female dancer, eine Tänzerin.* The precarious balancing act "on one toe" of this *Tänzerin* replaces what is apparently, for him, a more masculine "consciousness of unity and intimacy that should exist between author and work." With this gender shift in the authorial position of the writer, Freud introduces the final section of a text that will consist, in large part at least, of an impassioned defense of the role of the "great man" in history, in particular, of the uniquely great man Moses, who, Freud will not hesitate to assert, "made" and "created" the Jewish people: "It was the single man, Moses, who made the Jewish people."[5]

Despite this defense of the historical significance of great men, certain feminine traces appear in their shadow, barely visible but still legible: the ballerina to whom Freud compares himself as writer, balancing on one toe; Akhenaton's mother, who possibly introduced him to the idea of a single deity;[6] the Midianite wife of Moses, who saves him from the wrath of Yahweh by circumcising their son in the nick of time. These three feminine figures make up the shadowy supporting cast of what Freud, in a famous letter to Arnold Zweig (written in 1932), called his "historical novel."[7] And yet, since this is a text as much about disappearance as appearance, as much about ghosts as about living persons, a text traversed by revenants, doubles, and splits, such shadowy figures acquire a significance that far exceeds the bit—and silent—parts these "extras" are assigned to play. The essay itself, Freud acknowledges in his introduction to the final section, has taken on something of the quality of a revenant: "In truth it has been written twice over. The first time was a few years ago in Vienna, where I did not believe in the possibility of publishing it. I decided to put it away, but it haunted me like an unredeemed spirit [*ein unerlöster Geist*], and I compromised by publishing two parts of the book independently in the periodical *Imago*" (132/211). If the book was written and finally published as a whole, as a work, in order to put its "unredeemed spirit" to rest, the question of just how far it succeeds remains open. Having definitively left the country of his birth and gone into exile, Freud writes:

> I found the temptation irresistible to make my withheld knowledge accessible to the world . . . , and so I started to rewrite the third part of my essay, to follow the two already published. This naturally necessitated a partial reorganization of the material. But I was not able to integrate [*unterzubringen*] the whole material [*den ganzen Stoff*] into this second revision [*in dieser zweiten Bearbeitung*]. Nevertheless, I could not entirely give up the earlier versions. (132/211)

A certain attachment to the past—which is to say, to the "unredeemed spirit"—thus prevents Freud from fully integrating past versions into the "second revision." The result is that this "second revision" has the effect of calling the sovereign power of the author over his work into question: "The creative force of an author unfortunately does not always follow his will; the work grows as it will and often it confronts the author as though it were independent, indeed even alien" (133/211).

From an aesthetic and indeed intellectual point of view, Freud regards this result as problematic. And yet from a psychoanalytical standpoint, it is both familiar and significant. Freud's text resists submission to a "second revision"—*eine[r] zweite[n] Bearbeitung*—that would complete it and make it meaningful. But as he had explained in the *Interpretation of Dreams*, the meanings produced by "secondary revision [*sekundäre Bearbeitung*]" are designed to conceal the true significance of the dream. Secondary revision attempts to "distort the distortion" of the other elements of the "dream-work" and thereby to mask the conflicts of desire that the dream both articulates and dissimulates: articulates *by* dissimulating. What Freud does not say explicitly, but what his text shows, is that the form employed by secondary revision to render the dream-text ostensibly transparent is that of a continuous *plot* or *story-line*, with beginning, middle, and end. The returns, redundancies, and contradictions of which the author regretfully takes note disrupt just such narrative continuity and consistency. "Secondary revision," of course, was meant to apply only to products of the unconscious, such as dreams, not to psychoanalytic essays seeking to comprehend dreams, fantasies, or, in this case, historical reality and its legends. Or could it be that the line between these different domains is not as clear-cut as one might expect?

The Man

Those familiar with the German text will recognize that the English title takes two liberties with Freud's German. First, it condenses *monotheistische Religion* into the single word *Monotheism*. Although this is not without consequences, to which I will return shortly, they are probably less significant than the second liberty taken with the title. This involves the pure and simple omission of Freud's designation of Moses as a "man": *Der Mann Moses und die monotheistische Religion*. "Man" here means at least two things. First, it means that Moses was human and not divine. Indeed, as we have already indicated, Freud argues that Moses, as a "great man," stood "behind" the idea of the God of the Jews: the great man was father of the God and not just

His prophet; Creator of the Jewish people and not just its leader (its *Führer*[8]). But, and this is crucial, the great man was still human, and as such, he was mortal. It is not easy, and perhaps impossible, to kill a God. But it is relatively easy, according to Freud at least, to kill a man. The problem, as we have seen, is "doing away with the traces." The English translation of Freud's title tends to cover up at least some of these traces by effacing the attribute *man* from the proper, or not so proper, name *Moses*. And yet Freud insists that, if Moses was no doubt a "great man," he was nonetheless human. As a human being, he was mortal. But, and this brings us to the second point, as a human being he was also gendered. He was the founder of a religion and the leader of a people, but he was also a father, and, like every father, he had once upon a time also been a son. Freud warns against the danger of forgetting this simple, yet complicated fact:

> When . . . the figure of the great man has grown into a divine one, it is time to remember . . . that the father too was once a child. The great religious idea for which the man Moses stood was, as I have stated, not his own; he had taken it over from his King Akhenaton. And the latter—whose greatness as a founder of religion is proven beyond a doubt—perhaps followed intimations which through his mother or by other ways had reached him from the Near or the Far East.
>
> We cannot trace the network any further. (141/218)

To be "human," above all, a "man," may for Freud entail living in the shadow of the "great man" and, ultimately, of the primal "father." But to be human also means not to forget what cannot simply be remembered, namely, that the "father too was once a child" and that he cannot therefore, either as individual, fantasy, or position, be the absolute origin of everything that follows. To say that the idea of the One God is developed from the idea of the one and only Father is not just to replace one figure with another: it is to change the nature of the place itself. Instead of being the origin of a *creatio ex nihilo*, the irreducibility of the human, even in its paternal form, reinscribes that place into a "chain" or, as Freud corrects himself, into a "network"—one that can never be retraced to its absolute beginning or definitive end: "We cannot trace the network any further." Every place thus emerges as a re-placement of another place, every "here" as defined in relation to an elsewhere. And the nonfigure of this elsewhere, of this splitting of place, its not so much visible as legible trace, is *feminine*.

Thus the lack of a proper origin and of a proper end defines the "human" in this text as a network that eludes comprehension and thereby excludes appropriation. Akhenaton's monotheism, Freud notes, was no more "his own" than was that of Moses. And yet Freud introduces the hero of his novel by quoting Breasted, one of his scholarly sources, to the effect that Moses was "the first individual in human history" (21/118n.). Precisely the struggle between the establishment of a certain identity, individual and collective, and its disestablishment, distortion, and transformation is condensed in the ostensibly harmless concatenation of the "proper name" *Moses* and the generic noun *man*.

For these reasons, it is regrettable that the English translator, with or without the approval of Freud,[9] decided to omit the attribute *man* from the title of this text. This omission, together with that of the noun that concludes Freud's title, namely, *religion*, effaces the space within which Freud's text takes place—between *man* and *religion*, between the *human* and the *divine*, between the *masculine* and the *feminine*, between *mortality* and *survival*, and, perhaps most importantly of all, between the *network* and the *work*. In renaming *The Man Moses and Monotheistic Religion* as *Moses and Monotheism*, the English translator gave Freud's text the semblance of a unified *work*, but at the expense of obscuring its complexity as a heterogeneous *network*. The ostensibly proper name *Moses* appears as the ground and goal of the essay, but only through erasure of its defining attribute: the generic noun *man*.

One instance can stand for many: the long discussions about the force of "tradition" in history and the role that "great men" play in it. Since even the "greatest" of men, the most heroic or memorable, still remains a finite being, the question of his role in constituting such a tradition is posed. This question becomes especially acute when the tradition involved is succeeded by another one that claims to be founded by a human who is also the son of God. Freud spends pages discussing the conditions under which a mortal individual such as Moses could participate in transmitting and establishing a heritage that has endured for thousands of years. One aspect of the response he provides to this question is that the ability of an individual to transcend the limitations of finitude is related to *a particular experience of mortality.*

In order to discuss just what that experience entails, it will be helpful to recall, briefly, certain aspects of the story that Freud unfolds in his "historical novel." The book published in German as *The Man Moses and Monotheistic Religion* consists of three separate but interrelated texts. The titles of the individual essays are precise and to the point. The first, "Moses an Egyptian," takes up existing arguments that Moses was of Egyptian origin and adds to them a specifically psychoanalytical one, drawn from Otto Rank's *The Birth of the Hero*, which establishes a pattern in the "exposure [*Aussetzung*]" and abandonment of the hero as an infant. The biblical account, of course, depicts Moses as the child of modest Levites, who, after being abandoned, is adopted and raised by the daughter of the Pharaoh. This version diverges from the usual exposure myth as reconstructed by Rank in that it depicts Moses' real family as being of humble origin and his adoptive family as being noble. In this variation Freud sees possible support for the hypothesis that Moses was indeed of Egyptian origin, and that therefore he had to "descend," socially and culturally, in order to become the leader of the Jews. Perhaps more significant is the fact that this hypothesis amounts to dispossessing a people of its founder and, in a certain sense, of its origin. The origin of the Jewish people, insofar as it resides in the Mosaic religion, is, Freud argues, external and extrinsic: it is, in the strict sense, *heterogeneous.* The origin of the "nation" would thus consist not in its "nativity," not in a continuity of life expressed in blood and birth, but in that which follows, both individually and collectively. The identity of a people, of a nation, at least in the specific case of the Jews, comes to it from afar. It is acquired, not innate.

Yet only in the second essay, "If Moses Was an Egyptian . . . ," does Freud begin to elaborate some of the consequences of this initial hypothesis, indeed, some of the historical arguments that might support it. Of particular interest are the three dots that both close and open the title of this section: "If Moses was an Egyptian," they seem to say, "what *then*?" The ellipsis signifies something omitted, left out. Despite everything that will flow from Freud's pen in response to that question, none of his conclusions will ever entirely fill up the gap opened by those three dots, which could also be seen as a proliferation of periods, but which, in their repetition, underscore the incompleteness of the title phrase.

Freud unfolds the consequences and ramifications of those three elliptical dots in seven sections, like the seven days of the week, or of the creation. But the world that emerges from these seven sections is very different from that depicted in Genesis. It is a world of conflict and compromises rather than of harmony and beatitude. It is also a world of singularities. Moses is designated as "*an* Egyptian." As usual, Freud's formulations cannot be taken too literally; he could have entitled this section, "If Moses Was Egyptian. . . ." Instead, he uses the indefinite article, thus giving the title the tone of a conjecture or hypothesis: *Wenn Moses* ein *Ägypter war. . . . If* Moses was *an* Egyptian, then he was not merely Egyptian in general, but rather a *certain kind* of Egyptian, one *among* others, but by no means one *equal* to all others.[10] Being a follower of Akhenaton, Moses, Freud argues, was the adherent of a radically new monotheistic religion introduced in Egypt by this Pharaoh, which, for a brief period, replaced the traditional polytheism that dominated the country before his reign and was restored soon afterward. Given the widespread opposition to the new religion, the only possibility of preserving this monotheism after Akhenaton's death, Freud speculates, was to transplant it outside of Egypt. This was the situation in which Moses "chose" the Jewish tribes living in Egypt to be the vehicle that would preserve the monotheism of Akhenaton by taking it out of the land of its origin. As Freud puts it, "it is possible that the religion that Moses gave his Jewish people was his own, *an* Egyptian religion although not *the* Egyptian religion" (21/118).

Later on, as we have already discussed, Freud will explicitly question or relativize Moses' "ownership" or property rights over the monotheistic religion that he asserts here. The paradox with which this essay struggles but which it never resolves is already clearly stated. The "monotheistic religion" that Moses brings the Jews is described as "his own," although it is clearly adopted from someone else, Akhenaton, who in turn received it from elsewhere. This is surely one of the most characteristic gestures of Freudian thought: wherever proper nouns reinforce the expectation that what they name is self-identical and unified, Freud finds splits and doubles, struggles and compromises. Instead of self-contained and meaningful *works*, he finds overdetermined and equivocal *networks*.

In this particular text the network *sets in* with the name *Moses* itself, in which Hebrew and Egyptian converge but also conflict,[11] and it extends from the name to the historical personage and to his religious and cultural significance. If Moses was an Egyptian, he was in profound and incompatible conflict with the dominant traditions of Egypt, and this and this alone sets the scene for the development of a Mosaic religion in exile, as it were, among the Jewish people. But the splitting and doubling go further and indeed emerge as the dominant structural characteristic of the story Freud unfolds in this second section. At the end of this section, he sums it up as follows:

> To express our result in the shortest formula: to the well-known dualities of [Jewish] history—*two* peoples that come together to form a nation, *two* kingdoms, into which this nation divides, *two* names of God in the source-writings of the Bible—we now add two new ones: *two* foundings of religions, the first repressed by the second but later reemerging victorious, and *two* religious founders, each with the same name, Moses, but whose personalities we must separate from one another. (64/154)

In a profound sense, Freud's entire interpretation in this essay—and doubtless elsewhere as well—is condensed in this summary: where a homogeneous and unified self-identity seems to hold sway ("the" Jewish people, "the" Egyptians, "Moses") Freud uncovers traces of a partially effaced story of splits and struggles. The key to understanding the emergence and survival of identity, whether individual or collective, resides in the configuration of traces left by such conflicting splits. This is why the lines that conclude the passage we have just cited take on a particular significance: "And all of these dualities are the necessary result of the first, the fact that the one component of the people had had an experience that must be deemed traumatic, which the other part was spared" (64–65/154). At the "origin" of the decisive "splits" and "dualities" is a traumatic experience, and not just any, but a very specific one: namely, the "cruel murder" of Moses by the people he had in a certain sense brought into being by bringing them the religion upon which their collective and enduring identity was to be based. The very people who owed their lives as a people, as a unified nation, to Moses, took his life cruelly, and this constitutes the traumatic origin that, for Freud at least, has determined the course of Jewish history and its traditions ever since. How such a traumatic "event" could in time come to shape a people is one of the major questions that Freud addresses in his third and final essay. But it in turn presupposes another, more general question, namely: In what does the actual nature of a tradition consist and on what is its power based?

Trauma and Tradition

The hypothesis of a possible murder of Moses by his people Freud found in a book published in 1922 by the Berlin archaeologist and biblical scholar Ernst Sellin, entitled *Moses and His Significance for the Israelite-Jewish History of Religion.* Without this source, Freud acknowledges, his essay "would have had to remain unwritten" (71/160). Freud summarizes Sellin's "discovery" as follows: "He found in the book of the prophet Hosea unmistakable traces of a tradition to the effect that the founder of [the Jewish] religion, Moses, met a violent end in a rebellion of his stubborn and refractory people. The religion he had instituted was at the same time abandoned" (42/136)."

But the abandonment of the religion of the founder was not to be definitive: "Toward the end of the Babylonian exile, the hope arose among the Jewish people that the man they had so callously murdered would return from the realm of the dead and lead his contrite people—and perhaps not only his people—into the land of eternal bliss. The palpable connections with the destiny of the Founder of a later religion do not lie in our present course" (42–43/136). Freud's attitude toward "historical research" is clearly demonstrated on this occasion. He does not endorse all aspects of Sellin's interpretation,[12] only his "decisive discovery." Why is this discovery so "decisive" for Freud? Primarily because it provides him with a serious scholarly endorsement of a hypothesis that he regarded as consistent with the theory of the murder of the primal father he had introduced many years before, in *Totem and Taboo*, and which in turn was intended as a prehistoric, anthropological confirmation of the Oedipal relation of father and son. Freud is moreover quite frank about his interest in adopting Sellin's assumption (*Annahme*), which, he writes, "allows us to spin our threads further, without contradicting trustworthy results of historical research. But independently of these authors, we still dare to "follow up our own trace [*einhertreten auf der eigenen Spur*]" (43/136–37). It seems, however, that what for Freud is "worthy of trust" or "belief"—*glaubwürdig*—is not so much historical research, which at best exercises a veto-power over his ability to hypothesize, but rather his desire to 'follow up his own trace,' that is, to continuing "spinning" the "threads" of his psychoanalytically oriented argument. To this end, it is indispensable, but also sufficient, to be able to *cite* at least one recognized scholarly source of Biblical scholarship to legitimate the hypothesis that Freud needs, namely that of the murder of Moses by his "own" people.[13]

There is another, equally important reason why this hypothesis—which, as Freud well knew, never succeeded in gaining wide acceptance in biblical scholarship—is so important for the argument of this essay. It allows Freud to address the one question that, as we have seen, overshadows all others in the third and final section: namely, the question of tradition, of historical transmission above and beyond the bounds of an individual life-span. In the passage just quoted, there is already an indication of this, in a second hypothesis that Freud takes over from Sellin: that of the murder of Moses as the origin of Jewish messianism. "A contrite people" would thus be "led into the land of eternal bliss" by their founder and leader, who, having been killed by them, would return from the dead to redeem his murderers. The trauma would thus return in the form of a messianic hope that both confirms the initial deed and at the same time, as we shall see, consummates it. Having taken the life of their leader, the Jews would constitute their collective identity through the messianic expectation of his redemptive return. Such a formulation is, to be sure, not to be found in Freud's text, but it nevertheless accurately describes Freud's conception of the originating trauma, the guilt it produces, and its transformation into a messianic hope that subsequently defines the relation of the Jewish people to its past, present, and future: that is, to its history. The decisive operator, here, is the middle term, *guilt,* which builds the bridge between past and future, between traumatic violence and messianic hope.

Reasoning, as so often, from his experience with individual neurotics, Freud construes the operation of such guilt on the model of repression, which, understood temporally, means the return of the repressed. In both individual and collective, he argues, repression and guilt organize the ambivalence of desire in a way that makes it compatible with the needs of identity formation.

But at the same time that he advances this analogy, Freud is also perfectly clear about its limitations. It is one thing to interpret the return of the repressed within the biographical continuum of an individual existence, however conflictual, and quite another to account for the effects of guilt in shaping the "tradition" of a community over a long period of time. Thus Freud acknowledges that

> the term "the repressed" is used by us here in an inauthentic sense. What is at stake is rather something gone

> by, gone missing [*Verschollenes*], overcome in the life of a people, which we dare to equate with the repressed in the psychic life of the individual. In what kind of psychological form this past was at hand during the time of its darkening [*Verdunkelung*] we cannot as yet say. (170/241)

This statement comes close to the end of the essay, and so Freud's acknowledgment that "we cannot *as yet* say" just what corresponds to repression in the history of a shared tradition leaves the reader with a question mark rather than a solution to the problem. This underscores the distinction between individual and collective experience. For the individual, repression consists in the replacement of an unacceptable representation by another one that is more acceptable—which of course means more acceptable to the *ego*. The repressed representation, which is denied access to consciousness, remains conserved in and as the unconscious, generally not as memory but as forgetting.[14] Where, however, not individuals but groups or collectives are concerned, the mechanisms of "replacement" and "conservation" no longer operate within the biological continuum of an individual life and within the horizon of its psychic counterpart, the ego. This is why the question that Freud poses at the end of his second essay, and with which the remainder of his text grapples without reaching a definitive conclusion, has to do with dimensions of experience that transcend the individual ego, namely, with the structure and power of "tradition," and with "trauma." When Freud tries to approach the question of tradition and how it differs from the "return of the repressed" in the individual, he uses two words that suggest a possible response. "What is at stake," he writes in German, is something *Verschollenes*, which took place during a period of *Verdunkelung*. Neither of these words belongs to the technical terminology of Freudian psychoanalysis. The first word, *Verschollenes*, will be familiar to readers of Kafka in German, since it recalls the recently restored title of his first novel, formerly known as *Amerika*. The novel has been retranslated into English as *The Man Who Disappeared*. Unfortunately, this translation omits two connotations of the German word *verschollen*, which are not without relevance to

Freud's use of it. First, "disappeared" suggests the negation of an appearance, and hence of something *visible*; the German word *verschollen*, however, is the past participle of the verb *verschallen*, which refers to an acoustical experience. A *Schall* is a sound, something that rings out, like "clanging cymbals" (or *Schall und Rauch*). Second, the experience referred to entails, not the negation of sound pure and simple, but rather its *fading away* or "dying out," an irreducibly *temporal* occurrence. In translating this I have therefore resorted to the British expression that retains this temporal aspect of passing away in the present: "gone missing."[15] In short, *Verschollenes* connotes not merely an *end result* but rather an ongoing *process* of ringing out, resounding, and in so doing fading away. A similar process is perhaps even more manifest in the second word mentioned, one whose ongoing, unfinished, and reiterative quality is reflected in its morphological form, which is that of the gerund: the word *Verdunkelung*, "darkening." Again, what is being described is less a state of being absent or becoming obscure than a process of *fading*, both visually and acoustically, and it is therefore all the more appropriate for something that resembles repression insofar as it marks the heightened effectiveness of the past in the present and for the future. The question of "tradition" thus has to do with making past experience transmissible. And the point of departure for this question is the recognition of a certain absence of knowledge: "In what psychological form this past was present at hand [*vorhanden*] during the time of its darkening, we cannot yet say."

But this absence of knowledge, this "growing faint [*Verschollenes*]" during a time of darkening (*Verdunkelung*) also applies to the "origin" of tradition in the traumatic event of killing the founding father. Wherein resides the "trauma" of this event? Although Freud is rather vague in his response, we can venture the following interpretation: The trauma resides in the incompatibility of the act with representational thinking, with the "stable cathexes" (*Besetzungen*: more literally, "occupations") associated with the self-perception of the ego, whether individual or collective. In killing Moses, his people brought his life to a "violent end." But through the aftermath of guilt, this "end" turns out to be the start of something else. Moses' life, as an individual, ended, but his significance for the people who killed him, was only beginning. In his being "shunted aside," done away with, traces were left that make their way.

Imagine That!

To retrace Freud's genealogy of trauma, guilt, and tradition in *The Man Moses*, we must return, not to the traumatic event itself—as if that were possible—but to the distinctive and significant way it is inscribed in this text. Its distinctive significance emerges perhaps most clearly if we compare it to its predecessor—its forefather, one might say—namely, the account of the murder of the primal father in *Totem and Taboo*: "One day the brothers who had been driven out came together, killed and devoured their father and thus put an end to the paternal horde. United, they dared and achieved what would have been impossible to them as individuals."[16]

The first and perhaps foremost difference between Freud's accounts of the killing of the primal father and of Moses is that in the latter text there is no semblance of a direct representation of the event, but only an allusion to the scholarly hypothesis of Sellin. In *Totem and Taboo*, by contrast, there is the fiction of a direct description. The passage that introduces it could not be clearer in this respect: "Let us imagine the spectacle of a totem meal," Freud urges his readers, as an introduction to the murder scene (176/174). Freud's German is even more direct: "Stellen wir uns vor," he begins his account, first of the totem meal, and then of the murder. The hypothesis is thus presented as a scene that can be visualized, depicted, and readers are invited to act as though they were viewers, spectators. The murder of Moses, by contrast, is presented from the start as inseparable from a nonvisualizable textual network. The biblical scholar Sellin is said to have found in the book of Hosea "unmistakable indications of a tradition, which has as its content" that Moses "found a violent end" at the hands of his own people. Freud will never ask his readers to imagine this event. In the case of Moses, at least, the traumatic killing seems to elude direct representation.

But this is only the initial difference between the two accounts. A second distinction, apparently unrelated to the first, has to do not with the mode of presentation but with the content. The father in the primal horde does not, in his immediate form at least, found a community or transform a people by giving it a new religion and taking it into exile to preserve it. Rather, he either subjugates or drives away all those who would make up such a community. There is no law in the primal horde other than the proprietary desires of the primal father. Community only begins with the "coming together" of the excluded in order to do away with the one who has cast them out. To be sure, this is then followed by a process of guilt and by a return of the repressed similar to that Freud finds at work in the aftermath of the murder of Moses.

The most striking difference between the two killings has to do, then, with their respective motivations. In the case of the primal father, it is the effort to break his stranglehold on all property, beginning with the women of the horde. In the case of Moses, the motivation is far less clear. Freud makes mention of the "stubborn and refractory" character of the people who commit the act. But stubbornness and refractoriness—*Widerspenstigkeit* and *Halsstarrigkeit*—seem hardly sufficient to motivate an act of this magnitude. And in fact Freud does not follow up this line of thought. What, after all, could the people be resisting?

The answer is perhaps nothing other than the religion Moses brought them or, rather, as Freud often writes, "imposed" upon them, albeit with their acquiescence, at the very least. This becomes clear when Freud adds that "at the same time" that Moses found a "violent end," "the religion he had imposed was cast off [*Gleichzeitig wurde die von ihm eingesetzte Religion abgeworfen*]. (42/136) This *Gleichzeitigkeit*, the *simultaneity* of the two acts, deserves our attention. The killing of Moses coincides, it would seem, with the "casting off" of the religion he had "imposed [*eingesetzt*]." It is this religion that was resisted and rejected by his "stubborn" people—not just rejected, but "cast off [*abgeworfen*]," the way one throws off a burden that has grown too heavy to bear. This is what the Egyptians had done after the death of Akhenaton, and it is what the Jews do after the death of Moses. What, however, was the burden that neither people could bear? Freud gives us an indication when he describes one of the reasons why the religion of Akhenaton never became popular in Egypt: "No other people of antiquity has done so much [as the Egyptians] to deny death, has made such careful provision for an afterlife; in accordance with this, the death-god Osiris, ruler of that other world, was the most popular and indisputable of all Egyptian gods" (20/117).

Whereas the Egyptians were content to wait until nature took its course to discharge themselves of this burden, the situation of the Jews was very different: "In both cases the same thing happened: those who felt themselves kept in tutelage, or who felt dispossessed, revolted and threw off the burden of a religion that had been forced on them. But while the tame Egyptians waited until fate had removed the sacred person of their Pharaoh, the savage Semites took their destiny into their own hands and did away with the tyrant" (58/148–49). In contrast to the Egyptians, the Jews took the matter of life and death into their own hands, by putting a "violent end" to the life of the prophet whose religion had, among other things, forbidden them all hope of representing a life beyond death, and thus of conceiving personal immortality. By doing away with the one responsible for this prohibition, the perpetrators could hope to deprive death of its radical alterity, survive it, and thereby domesticate it. By targeting Moses, they could ostensibly bring death back within the *scope* of representational thinking, action, and experience.

I use the word *scope* here advisedly. A certain scopic element remains associated with an unquestioned concept of representation. A "scope" requires a *target*. Again and again Freud problematizes this scopic experience, the experience of the spectator: for instance, in "our relation to death," as we have discussed in the preceding chapter, as well as in his interpretation of the "primal scene," where the position of the child as witness of parental coitus is only the beginning of a long sequence of aftereffects, which emerge belatedly, often after a period of "latency." Such belated aftereffects also follow upon the killing of Moses. These aftereffects do not consist, as I have already mentioned, in the straightforward return of the repressed. Neither Moses nor the unrepresentable deity of Mosaic religion ever simply "returns" once they have been cast off. Instead, as we have seen, their recurrence is marked by a certain splitting of form and figure: by divisions and doubles, either within a single proper name ("Moses," "Jewish People") or between names (Jahwe, Elohim, Adonai[17]).

What returns, above all, is a conflict in the definition of an identity that seeks to represent itself as being the *one and only*, over and above its relation to any other: as the one and only universal deity; as the one and only chosen people; as the one and only life seeking to define itself through its demarcation from death as its symmetrical and subordinate other.

In this perspective, a certain pleasure can be taken in the acting-out of such a demarcation by putting an end to the life of another and thereby subordinating life in its individual manifestations to a teleological-representational framework within which the *end*, death, is made meaningful as a *goal*. This process can be summed up as *targeting*. Moses is targeted so that his killers can live—which is to say, survive his death. But the target does not simply disappear. The murder of Moses is not the end of Freud's "historical novel," but rather the beginning of its afterlife, something less visible but still legible: the beginning not of a *novel* but of a *network*, one that is discontinuous, repetitive, recurrent and perhaps above all, unpredictable. Its end is never in sight. But what, then, of its beginning?

The One and the Other

In one of the countless "repetitions" that traverse this text, Freud explains the mechanism of "repression": "What is forgotten is not erased, but only 'repressed,' its memory-traces are present in all their freshness, but by means of 'counter-cathexes' *isolated*. They cannot enter into circulation with other intellectual processes, are unconscious, inaccessible to consciousness" (120–21/201). This all sounds familiar enough. And yet in this repetition there is a difference worth remarking. In order to "explain" repression, Freud here invokes a concept introduced a decade earlier, in *Inhibition, Symptom and Anxiety* (1926): that of *isolation*. Whereas in the earlier essay Freud had taken pains to distinguish isolation from repression, he now uses it to define the process itself. In other words, *isolation* no longer appears as one defense mechanism among others, alongside repression, as it were, but as its essence. Thus, if repression operates by withholding representations from consciousness and replacing them with surrogates, the process of withholding functions by "isolating" individual representations so that they can no longer "enter into circulation" with others. Repression is thereby described as an interruption or suspension of circulation (*Verkehr*: traffic). Freud actually contrasts "isolation" with "repression" by emphasizing that "isolation" achieves the same result as repression, but without rendering the representations it isolates inaccessible to consciousness: Isolation does not have to do this, since the problematic significance of the representation can be rendered acceptable to the ego simply by being denied contact with other representations. In his discussion of this process in the earlier essay, Freud emphasizes that it is extremely difficult to distinguish the neurotic, pathogenic aspect of "isolation" from normal, everyday thought, since what it does—stripping or excluding the ramifications from the object or node from which they proceed—so closely resembles "the normal process of concentration."[18] He continues:

> Whatever seems to us to be significant as an impression or as a task should thus be protected against disturbances through the simultaneous claims of other intellectual agencies or activities. But already in normal life concentration is used to keep away not only things that are indifferent or irrelevant, but above all oppositions that don't fit in [*das unpassende Gegensätzliche*]. What is felt to be most disturbing of all are those things that originally belonged together but which through developmental progress have been torn asunder [*auseinandergerissen*], for instance expressions of the ambivalent father-complex in our relation to God.[19]

The last remark suggests how pertinent the notion of *isolation* is to Freud's discussion in *The Man Moses.* The tension in Freud's own text between the novelistic concentration upon a "great man," Moses, and the continued demonstration that his historical role requires a complex and variegated *network* that cannot be reduced to or comprehended within the parameters of a single individual crystallizes in the "act" by which the hero is murdered by the people he "created." In his discussion of "isolation" in the earlier text, Freud emphasizes that it must be conceived not merely as an intellectual activity affecting mental representations, *Vorstellungen,* but rather as a process whose significance is modeled upon "the motoric sphere": "After an activity that possesses a neurotic significance, a pause is interjected [*eingeschoben*], in which nothing more is allowed to happen, no perception made and no action performed" (150–51). This physical and spatial "dimension" introduces an interval or distance between the isolated object and its implications, its ramifications, and the general relational network in which it is not only "inscribed" and "situated," but endowed with "significance"—neurotic or otherwise. Freud is thus describing the passage from *significant, differential relations, implying a network or text,* to *objectification, implying a self-contained and unified object, and above all, subject*: in Freudian terms, an *ego.* But since the object depends upon the relations it excludes, it tends to threaten the stability of that ego, which requires a self-contained object in order to maintain itself. The "resolution" of this tension takes the form of "targeting," which seeks to identify, localize, and "do away" once and for all with the target. Hitting the target and doing away with the object are thus designed to confirm the subject as that which through the process confirms its ability to survive and remain the same.

The act of targeting, especially when linked to killing, introduces an irreducible pause or interval that frames the being it simultaneously encloses and arrests. When Moses is targeted, he as an individual is both done away with, finished off, and at the same time forever isolated in his martyrdom. Yet the very act that seeks to isolate the figure of Moses prepares the way for his return and proliferation, beginning with a hypothetical second

Moses (the Midianite Moses) and continuing with the prophets, in whom Freud sees the true heirs and guardians of the Mosaic tradition. The "isolation" and targeting of Moses thus affirms the autonomy of a single figure and positions it to serve as model for a notion of collective identity based on the self-perception of the ego. But this identity can maintain itself historically, which is to say, above and beyond the limits of individual finitude, only through the power of guilt, through which trauma is transformed into tradition. The trauma consists not in the murder of Moses per se but in the double bind it creates: Moses is murdered in order for the people he created to survive or, rather, to retain faith in their collective capacity to survive. But in "doing away" with the figure of the founder, this people also undercuts the model of its very identity insofar as the latter is understood "egologically," which is to say, as *one and the same*. This is why the figure of Moses must be reinstated, repeated, and resurrected through *guilt*. In German, as Nietzsche emphasized in the *Genealogy of Morals,* the word *Schuld* means not just guilt but also debt (*Schulden*). Nietzsche thereby restores "circulation" to a word whose significance has been "isolated" and reduced to a univocal meaning, namely that of moral culpability. To be "guilty" is thus not to have done something wrong but to be obligated to others. Indeed, perhaps the former is only a special case of the latter.

The form this assumes in Freud's text is that of the "compromise" by which the repressed is compelled to admit other elements in order to operate its "return." Freud even sees in this process a fundamental predilection of history itself: "History loves such restorations, in which belated fusions are undone and earlier separations reemerge" (137/44). Freud clearly sees his own text as bringing this "love" of history to the fore. What he does not emphasize is that the "earlier separations" are not composed of discrete, self-contained entities, but are rather already spinoffs of earlier "fusions."

Perhaps this is why Freud in this text continually associates the advent of "trauma" with the period in which the individual is just beginning to acquire the ability to speak ("der Zeit der beginnenden Sprachfähigkeit," 179/93). This ability, as we know from other writings of Freud,[20] is essential to the capacity of the ego to establish stable "cathexes." In its initial stage, however, verbal ability—which can also be equated with the ability to isolate—has not yet been fully developed. The experiences that provide the trauma with its material and medium are, Freud argues, primarily either "experiences on one's own body or sense-perceptions" (179/93). But since the ability to preserve such experiences or perceptions in an identical state over time is still relatively weak, the body and perception cannot yet be taken for granted as media for the constitution of self-identity. This requires a prolonged period of linguistic and symbolic acquisition, which perhaps is what explains the "latency" period, at least from a Freudian point of view. The "latency period" permits the ego to stabilize itself sufficiently, through the acquisition of linguistic and symbolic systems, to reintegrate the repressed trauma, though in the form of isolated events and figures, "screen memories." What they would screen out is the "network" or, rather, its *netting*, in the sense previously described. And they would do this by superimposing upon it a self-contained, linear narrative structure often associated with the novel, with beginning, middle, and end, capable of being taken in by the spectator-subject, who would thus find solace in "surviving" the end of the story as the end of the other.

Removing the Traces

As the remark of Walter Benjamin quoted at the outset suggests, a certain pleasure in the idea of killing can thus be related to the relief of reading about deaths the reader hopes to survive. Such reading is tantamount to a certain kind of "seeing"—from the secure distance of a detached and omniscient observer. At the end of the story, death is thus *seen* to befall others, while the reader lives on to retell or reread the story. The visible end of the hero, or of the enemy, can thus be taken to define the distance that the spectator hopes will protect him from a similar fate.

It is precisely this ostensibly protective distance that the "network" of Freud's writings tends to undermine, by reinscribing finite marks—whether of names or of persons—into relationships whose singularity can never be univocally identified, stabilized, and domesticated. As with the name *Moses*, the significance of such relationships cannot be ascribed to a single people, whether Jewish, Egyptian, Assyrian, or other—nor to a single person, nor even to a single gender. And yet, *because* these marks can never be domesticated or named properly, they incessantly provoke the desire that Freud's text both *describes* and *acts out*, a desire that overshadows all identity and identification, whether individual or collective, religious or secular: the desire to target, to isolate, identify, and "cast off" the burden of a world whose heterogeneous networks elude and undo all efforts to represent and comprehend them.

Paradoxically or, perhaps more precisely, *ambivalently*, this desire to *cast off* what in Freud's text functions as the origin of a *tradition* will impose a new series of constraints and burdens upon those it *subjects*: that is, subordinates but also subjectifies. In "doing away with" Moses, his killers bind themselves, and even more their descendants, to the network in which Moses is already inscribed. As previously suggested, this binding is the result of a sentiment of "guilt," *Schuld*, which also entails the *acknowledgment*, but not necessarily the *knowledge*, of *obligations* or *indebtedness*. How such obligations are transmitted from one individual to another—how, in short, individual guilt becomes collective tradition—is a question that Freud never fully answers, in this essay or elsewhere. But his text nevertheless points in a direction that he himself could no longer pursue. While he *asserts* the "phylogenetic" basis for tradition, what Freud *describes* is something quite different:

> There seems here to be a clear case [*ein gesicherter Fall*] of archaic heritage deriving from the time of the development of language, but one could also attempt another explanation. One could say that it is a question of the thought-relation between representations that had emerged during the historical development of language and that now have to be repeated each time that linguistic development is traversed individually. It would then be a

> case of the inheriting of a thought disposition [*Denkdisposition*] just like a drive-disposition [*Triebdisposition*] and once again [*wiederum*] no new contribution to our problem. (126/206)

Although Freud goes on to assert that not just "dispositions" but "contents [*Inhalte*] transmitted through "memory-traces of the experiences of earlier generations" constitute tradition, the only conceivable *medium of transmission* remains that of *language*, in particular, of individual languages, in which *systematic codification of meaning* is always at odds with the over-determined virtuality of signification. Language thus both *poses* and *disposes*, not just semantically but syntactically. Such conflicts and tensions play themselves out in the ambiguities attached to nouns and to names, and above all to their pretension of being "proper," that is, of representing or designating *univocally*. This is what is at stake in the targeting of the "man Moses," who, we recall, was "*an* Egyptian," "*one* Egyptian" but not "(*the*) Egyptian" per se. Moses was "an Egyptian" in assuming his difference not just from other Egyptians but from himself. This self-differentiation or, better, self-deferral, this separation from and *parting with oneself*, resists representation in Freud's account of the very act meant to "do away with" its ban. Instead of simply "doing away" with its target, it shunts it aside, and in so doing succeeds where it fails and fails where it succeeds. This dual destiny reveals retroactively the uncontrollable and unpredictable aftereffects of lethal targeting: in seeking to cast off the net, it ensnares itself all the more in its coils.

CHAPTER

5

Networks, Netwar, and Narratives

> What is most fascinating about the developments taking place at the cutting edge of military formation at the beginning of the twenty-first century is therefore this. The very means by which phenomenality is itself en-gendered—the intimate correlation between appearing and what appears, enacted through the power of signification—has become, above all, the prowess to which martial embodiment, paradigmatically represented by the United States military, now aspires. Strictly speaking, the contemporary military body is no longer a mere "formation." It frankly recognizes itself to be "in-formation." The word play is deliberate and revealing. A creature of the age of information and code, it espouses the view that the very power of en-gendering—en-gendering itself—is, fundamentally, a function of code, subject via digitalization and geneticization to electronic and molecular modulation and control. It embraces the allied view that, as a function of code, any (military) body must be endlessly mutable, and that the way to command this mutability is to develop a strategic virtuosity in the employment of information in order to refashion (military) bodies-in-formation according to any and every eventuality. Having cracked the code, military corporeality now embraces martial becoming.
>
> Michael Dillon and Julian Reid, *The Liberal Way of War*

If Freud's two essays, written in the midst of the First World War and on the eve of the Second, clearly belong to a single epoch, the military and strategic thinking being elaborated at the start of the twenty-first century would seem, at first sight, at least, to be part of a different world. And yet, however striking and undisputable the differences that separate the two worlds may be, they also set off certain shared concerns, concepts, and paradigms. Not the least of these has to do with a sense of epochal transformation. This situation is complicated by the fact that for Freud, as for Nietzsche before him, the epoch that was drawing to a close had placed its trust in and indeed defined itself through its faith in history as a progression of autonomy and rationality. This belief in historical progress, for Freud and many others, did not survive the shock of "wartime"—of the "Great War" and its aftermath. Freud did not live to see the worst horrors of the Second World War, although, as his writings show, he would hardly have been surprised by them. But even for less pessimistic—or should one say realistic—observers, the spread of genocidal destruction associated with two world wars, but also with the colonial and imperialist policies of the "civilized" countries before *and after*, notions such as "progress" have today been largely supplanted by terms that strive to appear more neutral, such as "transformation," while an emphasis on technological, biological and other determinisms has tended to supplement, if not replace, hopes previously vested in values such as "humanity" and "civilization."

To replace notions such as the "historical progress of mankind" or of "civilization" with the insistence on bio-technical determinism reflects both the "disillusion" of which Freud wrote and the effort to save what Freud had considered the cause and object of that disillusion: the belief in historical change as a teleological movement. To be sure, this requires a shift in tone, of which the following is an interesting example:

> Nearly all nations are moving from the industrial age to the information age. One of the tenets characterizing entry into the information age is the plummeting cost of very high quality information technology. Virtually ubiquitous, this equipment is broadly available and you do not

> have to be one of the leading world economies in order to have access to very advanced technologies. All of the major technological advances, energetics, propulsion, explosives, bio-engineering, are all achieved by virtue of information. As we move into this new age there are new rules that emerge, new power centers, new relationships and people behave in different ways. These are very profound changes.[1]

By replacing "civilization" with "information," "man" with "technology" and "history" with economics, the validity of enlightenment universalism seems to be confirmed: technological transformations are said to make "entry into the information age . . . broadly available" by virtue of "the plummeting cost of" such technology. "New rules" emerge, which replace old laws; "new power centers" replace older political entities; "new relationships" and new modes of behavior, individual and collective, replace "society" and its subcategories: classes, groups, clans. Conclusion: "People behave in different ways"—different from each other and different from the past. "These," we are told, add up to "very profound changes." However, we need only follow this passage to its conclusion in order to discover that the consequences drawn from these "profound changes" are not quite what the previous remarks might have led readers to expect: "These are very profound changes. The United States has been in a leadership position and this is not a position that we can or should give up. This is a wholly changed strategic development" (ibid.).

People may behave in different ways, and very profound changes may have taken place, but one thing is to remain unchanged: the "leadership position" of the United States, which is not negotiable: "not a position that we can or should give up." And the fact that this aspect of the past should also determine the future is precisely what constitutes the most important change of all: "This is a wholly changed strategic development." Nations may come and go, but one nation is to reign—and *remain*—supreme.

The author of these observations is retired Admiral Arthur

K. Cebrowski, who, after a distinguished career in the U.S. Navy, was named by the Donald Rumsfeld in 2001 to serve as director of the newly founded Office of Force Transformation, reporting directly to the secretary of defense. In the interview from which these remarks are taken, dating from October 2002, Admiral Cebrowski introduces these observations with the following caveat, which makes clear the urgent need for the newly created office that he leads: "The United States is the big kid on the block. Everyone else studies us. Everyone else designs against us. As a consequence . . . to the extent that America does not transform, its military force is ultimately doomed. That is because while we now occupy a far superior military position, the rest of the world is changing and what constitutes superior military positioning is equally likely to change" (ibid.).

America must change its ways, or its military superiority and its political supremacy are doomed. One month before Admiral Cebrowski gave this interview, in September 2002, the United States government issued its "National Security Strategy" report, which placed Admiral Cebrowski's caveat in a wider historical perspective: that of a caveat *preemptor.* Beginning with the conviction that "The United States possesses unprecedented—and unequaled—strength and influence in the world," the report contrasts the dangers and challenges of the post–cold war period:

> It has taken almost a decade for us to comprehend the true nature of this new threat. Given the goals of rogue states and terrorists, the United States can no longer solely rely on a reactive posture as we have in the past. . . . We cannot let our enemies strike first. . . . To forestall or prevent such hostile acts by our adversaries, the United States will, if necessary, act preemptively.
>
> In exercising our leadership, we will respect the values, judgment, and interests of our friends and partners. Still, we will be prepared to act apart when our interests and unique responsibilities require. [2]

This statement marked a radical transformation in official American foreign policy, consisting in the abandonment of the "cold war" strategy of multilateral deterrence, which, however often it had been ignored in practice, had nonetheless still been accepted by postwar American governments as a basic principle in dealing with other nations. The new document still paid lip-service to the notion of "balance of power," although attention to linguistic detail suggests that a very different approach was in fact at work here. Thus, President George W. Bush, in his statement introducing the document, stressed that "In keeping with our heritage and principles, we do not use our strength to press for unilateral advantage. We seek instead *to create* a balance of power that favors human freedom" (1, my emphasis). A "balance of power," however, is not generally considered to be something that can be "created" but at most *maintained*, since precisely as a *balance* it presupposes a certain equality among the elements comprising it. The notion of *creation*, by contrast, however secularized it has become over the past centuries, still remains indebted to its theological origins, and hence implies a certain transcendence or exceptionality. "To create a balance of power" suggests that there was no such balance previously and that it must be brought into being. And the manner of such a creation will have to be precisely that which the passage above begins by disavowing: namely, "unilateral" action. Whatever is created has to be created unilaterally. Between the Created and the Creator there can never be a "balance of power."[3]

And yet, although these three tenets constitute at the very least a change in the strategy of American foreign policy, they can also be seen as a continuation of one of its most powerful traditions: the doctrine of American exceptionalism, in which the moral superiority of a "manifest destiny" is associated with an uncontested military and technological *supremacy*. At the same time, something like a dialectics of power remains the justification of the new strategy. Global political *supremacy*, understood in large measure to derive from economic and technological superiority, is at the same time declared to be *supremely vulnerable*, given the relative availability of destructive technology to "rogue states" and, perhaps even worse, to nonstate "terrorist" groups. As President Bush puts it, again in his introductory remarks:

> Defending our Nation against its enemies is the first and fundamental commitment of the Federal Government. Today, that task has changed dramatically.[4] Enemies in the past needed great armies and great industrial capabilities to endanger America. Now, *shadowy networks* of individuals can bring great chaos and suffering to our shores for less than it costs to purchase a single tank. Terrorists are organized to penetrate open societies and to turn the power of modern technologies against us. . . .
>
> As a matter of common sense and self-defense, America will act against such emerging threats before they are fully formed. . . . History will judge harshly those who saw this coming danger but failed to act. In the new world we have entered, the only path to peace and security is the path of action.[5]

Given the "shadowy" nature of those elusive "networks," it is only "common sense" that the "path of action" must be "proactive"—a word not used in this document, but which in its widespread currency today indicates the solidarity of the new political and military rhetoric with the discourse of business management and its avatars.[6]

The new policy of military supremacy, to be enforced, if necessary, by proactive, that is, preemptive and unilateral action, has a history that roughly parallels that with which we are concerned here, that of "netwar." Although the search for origins is always hazardous, an early articulation of the doctrine of American supremacy can be found in a book published in 1998 by Zbigniew Brzezinski, then national security advisor to President Jimmy Carter, under the title *The Grand Chessboard: American Primacy and Its Geostrategic Imperatives.*[7] In his book, Brzezinski defines the primary objectives of American foreign policy to be the economic subjugation of the Soviet Union and the control of central Asia and the Middle East. The attainment of these goals in turn demands policies that Brzezinski describes in terms that deliberately situate the new "geostrategy" as the present-day heir of Imperial Rome: "To put it in a terminology that harkens back to a more brutal age of ancient empires, the three grand imperatives of imperial geostrategy are to prevent collusion and maintain security dependency among the vassals, to keep tributaries pliant and protected, and to keep the barbarians from coming together.''[8]

Brzezinski's geopolitical strategy found a powerful echo and elaboration following the first Gulf War in 1991. One year later, in 1992, aides of then Secretary of Defense Dick Cheney, including Paul Wolfowitz, I. Lewis Libby, and Zalmay Khalilzad (currently ambassador to Afghanistan), prepared a draft of a document designed to provide a geopolitical framework for the assessment of military needs. This classified document, entitled ''Defense Planning Guidance,'' was leaked to the *New York Times* and *Washington Post*, and thus became the object of heated public discussion and criticism. It defined three major objectives of American foreign policy: first, preventing the emergence of any global *or regional* superpower capable of contesting American objectives; second, securing ''access to raw materials, primarily Persian Gulf Oil,'' as well as preventing the ''proliferation of weapons of mass destruction''; and third, the endorsement of unilateral military action as a means of attaining these goals. The controversy provoked by this draft was so great that Secretary Cheney was compelled to have it withdrawn and rewritten.

Although they did not become official policy at the time, the ideas formulated in this draft continued to make their way. One year later, in 1993, Andrew Marshall, an advisor both to Cheney and to leading Democrats, ''provided the incoming Clinton administration with a working paper that warned that Cold War weapons 'platforms' . . . were becoming obsolete in face of precision weapons and cruise missiles. Marshall instead proselytized for cheaper, quicker, smarter weapons that took full advantage of American leadership in information technology.''[9] Marshall also warned, however, that by developing such ''precision weapons'' America would force its enemies to rely on terrorist activities, which would be more ''difficult to target'' than traditional military formations.[10]

Brzezinski's 1997 book, the 1992 ''Defense Planning Guidance'' draft, and Marshall's 1993 working paper all helped shape the context of strategic thinking in which theories of "netwar" were to emerge. These are, then, relatively recent developments, scarcely a decade old. It is therefore hardly surprising that they have not as yet coalesced into anything like a coherent doctrine, much less a consistent concept. From the very first, however, the word has harbored two very different, if interrelated, tendencies. One is that of "Network Centered Warfare," more commonly designated through the abbreviation "NCW," initially associated with the author quoted at the outset, Vice Admiral Arthur Cebrowski, who, together with John Garstka, co-authored what is generally considered to be the paper that marked the emergence of NCW as an official military doctrine.[11] The other major use of the term, which goes back at least to 1993, is much broader in scope. In contrast to NCW, which is specifically aimed at developing military strategies and planning, *netwar* embraces the effects and potentialities of information networks upon conflicts *in general*, rather than just their military forms. Two of its best known practitioners are John Arquilla and David Ronfeldt, both researchers at the National Defense Research Institute of the RAND Corporation. In *Networks and Netwars*,[12] Arquilla and Ronfeldt take pains to distinguish their concept of *netwar* from its purely military homonym, which they prefer to designate "cyberwar":

> Back in 1992, while first wondering about . . . cyberwar as a looming mode of military conflict, we thought it would be a good idea to have a parallel concept about information-age conflict at the less military, low-intensity, more social end of the spectrum. The term we coined was *netwar,* largely because it resonated with the surety that the information revolution favored the rise of network forms of organization, doctrine, and strategy. Through netwar, numerous dispersed small groups using the latest communications technologies could act conjointly across great distances. We had in mind actors as diverse as transnational terrorists, criminals, and even radical activists. Some were already moving from hierarchical to new information-age network designs. (2)

Whereas "network centered warfare" designates the essentially *military* effort to adopt to changes in conflict deriving both from the use of computers in general, and in particular, from the shift in computing and organization that arose with the introduction of networks and the Internet, that is, the shift from "platform-centered" to a "network-centered" computing, the notion of *netwar*, as developed by Arquilla and Ronfeldt, has, despite its name, never been "centered" upon or restricted to "war" in the traditional, military sense. Rather, it embraces all forms of "network-based conflict and crime" that can be said to be "short of traditional military warfare." Thus, whereas discussions of "network centered warfare" tend to approach conflict from the perspective of the military institutions of the nation-state, discussions of "netwar" often focus upon nonstate "actors" and conflicts, while exploring ways in which the notion of "network" itself can be applied to nonmilitary conflict situations. In *Networks and Netwars,* for instance, Arquilla and Ronfeldt distinguish between three types of network: first, the *chain or line* network, which, as its name indicates, is organized in a linear, sequential manner, so that contact or communication travels from one node to another in a process that is construed as more or less fixed, or, as they write, "end to end"; second, the *hub, star, or wheel* network, in which the components of the network—which they often refer to as "actors"—"are tied to a central (but not hierarchical) node or actor" through which or whom all communication must pass; third, the *all-channel* or *full-matrix* network, in which elements are connected to one another *without* having to pass through a center (8). These three different types can of course be combined in various ways and in response to specific situations, but what they all have in common is that they are organized, although to different degrees, *horizontally* rather than vertically. This indicates that the most distinctive form of the network, by comparison to previous forms of organization, is the "all-channel" type, since it is least hierarchical and most dispersed: "Ideally, there is no single, central leadership, command, or headquarters—no precise heart or head that can be *targeted*. The network as a whole has little to no hierarchy: there may be multiple leaders.

Decision-making and operations are decentralized. . . . Thus the design may sometimes appear acephalous (headless), and at other times polycephalous (hydra-headed)."[13]

Note that the major change in warfare brought about by this type of network affects the nature of the *target*. It is no longer the "head" of the enemy group or organization, since the latter has no single head. With such proliferation, the very notion of "head" changes: The "all-channel" network is potentially either *acephalous* or *polycephalous* or a mixture of both. This trait can be extended to the phenomenon of netwar in general, which, the authors assert, "has two faces, like the Roman god Janus" (21). By this they refer to the moral and political ambiguity of "netwar," which can serve civil and "uncivil" society, criminal groups as well as those seeking social reform or revolution.[14] In this respect netwar might seem to be not so very different from traditional war. But the reference to Janus suggests something more complex, namely, that the *same* war can serve different purposes at what appears to be one and the same time. This implies, however, that the "one" time is not simply self-identical, not simply "one and the same." It thereby calls into question the relation between "war" and the structure of the "network," or indeed, as we shall see later on, between the "work" and the "net."

Already, however, it is clear that one of the traits that distinguishes traditional concepts of war from the notion of netwar elaborated by Arquilla and Ronfeldt is the relativization, although by no means elimination, of the vertical, hierarchical structures usually associated with the nation-state and in particular with its military and police institutions. It is precisely a certain "stasis" associated with those vertical military-political structures that, tendentially at least, is challenged by the horizontal organization of "netwar." This challenge does not simply entail the replacement of a centralized, hierarchical form of organization by a relatively decentralized, horizontal one. Rather, the very concept of "organization" changes. Arquilla and Ronfeldt stress the importance of this by insisting that, although "netwar" and "networks" are concepts that respond to developments in technology, and in particular, to information technology, they nevertheless must not be understood strictly in technological terms, but rather as a new "form of organization" (19). At the same time, while granting that the organization of networks cannot be isolated from its social context, the two researchers refuse to embrace an approach to networks and netwar that would be primarily either sociological or technological. One reason for this reluctance has to do with the need to elaborate concepts that are independent of previous disciplines in order to account for the distinctive characteristics and effects of networks and netwar.

Two of these concepts are "swarming" and "blurring," words that suggest the elusive and unstable movement and structures toward which networks tend. First, swarming: "Swarming occurs when the dispersed units of a network . . . converge on a target from multiple directions. The overall aim is *sustainable pulsing*—swarm networks must be able to coalesce rapidly and stealthily on a target, then dissever and redisperse, immediately ready to recombine for a new pulse" (12). This notion of "swarming" demonstrates that networked conflict can be distinguished from traditional military conflicts, and even from guerilla warfare, through its reliance upon the *dispersion* of force rather than upon its massing or concentration: the latter emerge as an effect of the former rather than the reverse. This predominance of dispersion can perhaps be generalized to characterize the network as a distinctive form of organization.

"Blurring" and "blending," by contrast, appear at first to be the opposite of "dispersion": in both, elements or operations are not "spaced out" extensively, but rather superimposed upon one another, thus "blurring" the distinction between "offense and defense," or blending "strategy and tactics" so that they can no longer be clearly distinguished from one another (13). What *blurring* and *blending* have in common with *swarming* is the tendency to suspend, up to a point, the oppositional logic of mutual exclusivity and hence also of the clear-cut distinctions informed by it. Such "blurring" of distinctions can, however, go further and affect not just the individual components or nodes of a network but the network itself, rendering its enabling limits difficult if not impossible to determine. This can result in a certain indeterminacy concerning the limits of the network, where it begins and ends, spatially as well as temporally.[15] Such indeterminacy can affect the conflicts in which the network engages. This is why, unlike traditional war, "netwar" requires no formal declaration to begin or to end, and why such declarations today seem increasingly superfluous even on the part of nation-states, as with recent U.S. military actions in Iraq or, going back further, Vietnam. At the same time, what stands out against this background of indeterminacy is the persistence of one notion that netwar shares with traditional war: that of *targeting*. However acephalous or Janus-faced netwar may be, there must still be an *enemy* to be *targeted*: which is to say, located and subdued, either by being killed, destroyed, or rendered dysfunctional or dependent. As we shall see, the notion of targeting plays a significant role in discussions of netwar.

This spatio-temporal dispersion and relative indeterminacy of both networks and netwar lead Arquilla and Ronfeldt, in the concluding chapter of *Networks and Netwars*, to pose a disarmingly simple but difficult question: "What holds a network together? What makes it function effectively?" "The answers," they respond, "involve much more than the organizational aspects emphasized" previously (323). Of course, they pose this question in the particular context of *netwar,* which involves a struggle to target, overcome, and neutralize adversaries in what is a more or less manifest conflict, if not an actually declared "war." Given the underlying structural transformations implied in network organization, and above all, what might be summarized as its underlying structural traits of *dispersion* and *mobility,* the question can be extended to other domains as well. What holds networks together? What is the relation of that "holding"—the cohesiveness of networks—to conflict? Is *targeting* something that occurs independently of the network or is it part and parcel of how the "net" works? If so, how then does a *net work* and what is involved in the association of these two rather different notions—*net* and *work*—to constitute what claims to be a single concept?

If the question of how a network holds together thus emerges as decisive, it is because traditional factors of organizational and structural cohesiveness can no longer be taken for granted. This is also what distinguishes the notion of a *network* from that of a *work tout court.* A work, at least as generally construed in the modern period, is the product of conscious, deliberate intent. It requires an "end" aimed at by a "head." In this perspective, a collective organization is often defined by reference to an animating, informing intention, a leading idea, principle or person—often all three convergent in a single figure. According to Arquilla and Ronfeldt, this configuration changes in netwar but by no means entirely disappears:

> In netwar, leadership remains important, even though the protagonists may make every effort to have a leaderless design. One way to accomplish this is to have many leaders diffused throughout the network who try to act in coordination, without central control or a hierarchy. This can create coordination problems—a typical weakness of network designs—but, as often noted, it can also obviate counter-leadership targeting. Perhaps a more significant, less noted point is that the kind of leader who may be most important for the development and conduct of a netwar is not the "great man" or the administrative leadership that people are accustomed to seeing, but rather the doctrinal leadership—the individual or set of individuals who, far from acting as commander, is in charge of shaping the flow of communications, the "story" expressing the netwar, and the doctrine guiding its strategy and tactics. (327)

Where networks lack a single center or leader, they are thus held together by "the narratives or stories that people tell" (328). If this is the case of other organizations as well, it is particularly important for networks that lack a "great man," a single heroic leader or leading idea. The question of a cohesive factor then becomes increasingly associated with the *stories* that hold together, or at least define, a network as a structure distinct from other, more hierarchical forms of organization. The ability to tell stories in turn involves the capacity to disseminate those stories—that is, to be heard, read, understood, and to convince those who are the "targets" of the stories, and thus the potential nodes or components of the network. And if the telling of stories plays a decisive role in the establishment of networks, then the means or medium by which such telling is disseminated will constitute an essential factor in the shaping and maintaining of networks.

This question could be pursued in a variety of directions. But to respond to the questions articulated, they would all have to relate the process of "telling" to the medium that allows it to be effective: the network and the work. The separation and thus delineation of the two can, in the history of Western modernity, be traced to the Reformation, and in particular, to the challenge it addressed to the traditional Catholic doctrine of the redemptive value of "good works," as well as the institution of the Church that the doctrine in part legitimated. In his study *The Origin of the German Mourning Play,*[16] Walter Benjamin examines this challenge to the authority of the Christian soteriological narrative—*Heilsgeschichte*—and its partial replacement by a theater staging death and destruction, the allegorical *Trauerspiel* or "mourning play." Benjamin emphasizes that the "mourning play" is *allegorical* insofar as the conventions in force prior to the Reformation—both theological and humanist—no longer provide an unchallenged principle of social cohesion and conventional meaning, because the *Heilsgeschichte* upon which they were based (even in their Renaissance, "secular" version) could no longer be taken for granted. Thus, baroque allegory, in contrast to its medieval predecessor, must be understood less as a "conventional expression" of meaning than as the "expression of [a] convention" that must be imposed. Such a convention cannot be regarded as (symbolically) meaningful, but only as (allegorically) *significant,* since the convention to which it appeals no longer exists in the form of a universal ("catholic") consensus. The theological and historical bases of that consensus have been shattered.

Hence, the authority of baroque allegory, which expresses itself theatrically rather than doctrinally, "is secret as to the dignity of its origin" but "public as to the range of its validity."[17] A corollary of this absence of an original, originating authority, in the political realm, is that the "sovereign," who no longer has the power or legitimacy to rule, and who no longer can produce great works, is increasingly overshadowed by the "plotter" (in German: *der Intrigant*). This plotter "plots," both in the sense of secretly manipulating and in that of spinning stories to obtain his end. Iago comes to mind, but also Hamlet, who, unable to assume the role of sovereign, schemes, stages, and sets traps in a vain attempt to reestablish an inaccessible legitimacy. In short, political power, usually associated with the executive, reveals a "telling" dependence upon disseminated narrative, which from now on, however—and this is its distinctly modern aspect—is associated with the medium of a certain theatricality, an allegorical theater. It is this medium, in all of its avowed inauthenticity—which Benjamin links to the "spatial simultaneity" of the stage (260)—that replaces the faltering eschatological medium of Christian *Heilsgeschichte*.

Yet Benjamin's account of the "origin" of this allegorical-medial theater, run by plotters rather than by legitimate sovereigns, still remains tied to a political structure, that of a court described as organized around a "figural center": "Allegory brings with it its own court; the profusion of emblems is grouped around a figural center [*figurales Zentrum*] that is never absent from genuine allegories."[18] The "center" described by Benjamin is "figural" insofar as the "court" that surrounds it is never fixed. The result is a certain *confusion* (Benjamin refers in this context to the title of a play by Lope de Vega, "The Confused Court"), since the elements that comprise it are brought together only to be dispersed once again: "'Dispersion' and 'Collection' ['*Zerstreuung' und 'Sammlung'*] are the laws of this court." Benjamin's discussion thus suggests that a certain spatio-temporal movement or, better, *rhythm* is built into the very structure of the court as allegorical-figural network.

Through its staging of suffering, murder, and death in the mourning play, this rhythm, which marks the recurrence of the "fall" rather than the coming of resurrection, endows the baroque network with relative stability and, indeed, endurance. But it is the stability and endurance of a shared guilt rather than the expectation of salvation. In this respect, Benjamin's analysis recalls, albeit in a very different vein, the importance that Freud attaches to guilt as a factor of social cohesion: by "doing away" with the "great man," the community of survivors is brought and held together by its collective sense of guilt—a sense that can be unconscious as well as conscious. Guilt serves to isolate the other as enemy, which is to say, as potential target to be hit and shunted to the side, *beseitigt*. Shoved aside, the target continues to mark the enabling limit of those who, by taking aim at it, hope to "do away with it" for good.

In short, something like targeting seems to be required to transform a net, which is to say, an indeterminable complex of relations, into a net-*work*, if by "work" is understood the self-contained object of a consciousness, the meaningful result of an intention, of a volitional and deliberate *act*. Targeting thus constitutes the condition of all *execution*, the execution of acts no less than that of judgments and sentences, such as the death-penalty. Every such execution, as targeting, is potentially and tendentially lethal, for by taking aim at its object, it isolates that object from its relation to its surroundings, removing everything that might *distract* its aim from the place it seeks to secure: that is, to occupy and to appropriate.

Since, however, the place targeted is always enmeshed in a net of relations that is intrinsically inexhaustible and unlimited, or, as Freud would say, *overdetermined*, the act of targeting is an act of violence even before any shot is fired. It is this act of violence that registers as "guilt"—which consists in the *denial of indebtedness* to an alterity without which nothing could be identified, no aim taken, no target hit. Thus, the execution of the act is undercut by precisely that which enables its performance, namely, "guilt." Guilt is what results from the impossible attempt to clear, occupy, and secure the place that would turn the *net* into a *work*, the *network* into a *people*, *nodes* into *great men*. Guilt, marking the *unacknowledged* debt to the other, to the *net without work*,[19] appears in Freud's text to serve as the glue that ultimately "holds together" the network, but only by dividing and deferring it through a "latency" period that endows it with an irreducible virtuality.

This virtuality is then articulated in legends and stories,

which could be grouped in two categories. First and most familiar are those that seek "redemption" from the obligations and ligatures of the *net* through the advent of a redeemer: eschatological or soteriological *Heilsgeschichten*, or their secular continuation in certain types of novels, which are perhaps the secular heirs of those *soteriological stories*, insofar as they seek to release their readers from the sense of being *trapped* in a network without discernible beginning or end. This at least is the function of the novel as described by Benjamin in his essay "The Teller" ("Der Erzähler"). Readers are drawn to such novels, he writes, "in the hope of warming their freezing lives on a death about which they read."[20] In other words, the end of the novel is read and experienced as if it were the overcoming of alterity through the represented death *of the other*; indeed, one could say that the other is targeted as the site of finitude, and this in turn allows the reader to draw solace from the sense of having survived the end, or at least being able to put down the book, stop reading, and still be alive.

The second narrative option, as delineated by Benjamin, offers no such totalizing conclusion. Instead, it always leaves room for the question "And what happened then?"[21] As a result, whereas "the reader of novels is solitary," the reader of and/or listener to stories remains in touch with a network of virtualities and latencies: "To tell stories is to continue to tell them [*sie weiter zu erzählen*]." That continuation, Benjamin stresses, requires memory and commemoration, *Erinnerung* and *Eingedenken*, but these in turn, as Freud (and before him, Nietzsche) reminds us, entail forgetting and foregoing, and thus inevitably also *Verschuldung*: indebtedness to what has been excluded in the process of filtering and selection, which, qua excluded, remains the telling limit of anything that can be told. This is why, as Benjamin writes with great precision, "memory founds the chain of tradition," but as a chain that is also a "net, which all stories form with each other in the end [*Erinnerung stiftet das Netz, welches alle Geschichten miteinander am Ende bilden*]."[22] Note that the stories described by Benjamin come together *in the end* to form a "net," but not a "network." The "end" of this net of stories is very different from that of the novel, which

Benjamin suggests is heir to the tradition of the epic. They involve different kinds of memories and different types of targets: "What emerges in this place is the opposition of the eternalizing memory of the novelist to the short-lived memory of the teller. The former is consecrated to the *one* hero, the *one* wandering journey [*Irrfahrt*], or the *one* battle; the latter, to the *many* dispersed events [*den* vielen *zerstreuten Begebenheiten*]."[23] *Schuld* interrupts and suspends the stories, framing them but never simply ending them; for "in the end" there is no way of definitively removing the "net": the many dispersed events, which cannot be gathered into any sort of definitive or conclusive unity. Precisely such a unity, by contrast, constitutes the end of the epic, according to Benjamin, and, by implication, of the novel. It targets "the one hero, the one journey, the one battle."[24]

Despite all their emphasis on "swarming" and "blurring," on leaderless, headless or polycentric structures, Arquilla and Ronfeldt's description of the cohesive function of narratives with respect to networks applies not to the tale but to the teleological tradition of the novel, as described by Benjamin, with its emphasis on unity and totality:

> Networks, like other forms of organization, are held together by the narratives, or stories, that people tell. The kind of successful narratives that we have in mind are not simply rhetoric—not simply a "line" or "spin" that is "scripted" for manipulative ends. Instead, these narratives provide a grounded expression of people's experiences, interests, and values. First of all, stories express a sense of identity and belonging—who "we" are, why we have come together, and what makes us different from "them." Second, stories communicate a sense of cause, purpose, and mission. They express aims and methods as well as cultural dispositions—what "we" believe in, and what we mean to do, and how.
>
> The right story can thus help keep people connected in a network whose looseness makes it difficult to prevent defection. The right story line can also help create bridges

> across different networks. The right story can also generate a perception that a movement has a winning momentum, that time is on its side. (328–29)

The "first" and primary function of narratives, according to this account, is to establish a clear-cut demarcation between *us* and *them,* between "who 'we' are . . . and what makes us different from 'them.'" And for any "movement" this can only mean getting "time on its side." The "solitude" of the novel reader is only apparently in contradiction with this collective determination, for the collective "us" so determined is one only by demarcation from "them," without whose contrasting foil "we" could never know "who we are" or "what we believe in." And the "sense of cause, purpose, and mission" that such narratives impart generates the "perception" that "time" is on the side of the perceiver.

Is it possible to conceive of a "movement" that would *net* rather than *network*, one which would leave room for the question that, for Benjamin at least, follows the end of every story—"And what happened next?" Or must that question always be targeted in advance by a preemptive answer? A concluding chapter will explore one possible response to this question.

CHAPTER

6

The Net and the Carpets

A situation with no way out produces guilt.
—Walter Benjamin, "Capitalism as Religion"

The Bottom Line

As we have seen, in his essay "The Teller" Walter Benjamin employs the figures of the "chain" and the "net" to distinguish the two major ways in which memory weaves tradition out of stories: "Memory establishes the chain [*Kette*] of tradition that leads from generation to generation [*von Geschlecht zu Geschlecht*]. It is the muse of epic in the largest sense. As muse, it determines the subspecies of the epic. Among these, the one that takes first place is that which is embodied in the storyteller. It establishes the net that all stories form with one another in the end."[1] The net that "all stories form with one another in the end" remains open, since the "end" always includes the responding question, "And what happened next?" Such memory is thus always directed not just to the past but to the future: to the future of the past, the aspect of what has been that has yet to be told. Benjamin designates this as "the short-lived memory of the teller" and contrasts it with "the eternalizing memory [*Gedächtnis*] of the novelist, which is informed by the search for unity: that of the "*one* hero, the *one* wandering journey, or the *one* battle." This distinction implies a very different position for both narrator and addressee. Whereas the unity of representation sought by the novelistic *Gedächtnis* presupposes a certain distance of the novelist from the events narrated, the "net" of stories allows no such distance for the teller of tales: "Tellers tend to begin their tales with an account of the conditions under which they themselves encountered that which is about to be told, if indeed they did not experience it directly" (447). In other words, the storyteller, in contra-distinction to the narrator of novels, begins by acknowledging and recounting the encounter with that which is about to be told.

An attachment of a very different sort, involving a very different kind of net, ushers in a short, unfinished text that Benjamin wrote in 1921, devoted not to a literary topic but to a political one: "Capitalism as Religion."[2] Even when one considers that Benjamin would have almost certainly never published the text in the form in which it has been included in his *Selected Writings*,[3] its beginning has to be deemed one of the most remarkable and most singular in all of his writing:

> Capitalism must be seen as a religion, i.e. capitalism serves essentially to allay the same cares, torments, troubles to which in the past the so-called religions offered answers. To demonstrate [*Nachweis*] how this religious structure of capitalism is not merely religiously conditioned, as [Max] Weber thought, but rather an essentially religious phenomenon, would even today lead us astray, down the path [*auf dem Abweg*] of measureless universal polemics. We cannot draw closed the net in which we stand [*Wir können das Netz in dem wir stehen nicht zuziehen*]. Later however an overview will be possible. [*Später wird dies jedoch überblickt werden.*] (288/100)

The text begins with an assertion that seems clear enough: In contra-distinction to the well-known thesis of Max Weber in *The Protestant Ethic and the Spirit of Capitalism,* Benjamin states that capitalism must be considered not merely as the result or effect of a religion, as "conditioned" by it, but rather as itself a religious manifestation responding "essentially" to "the same cares, torments, troubles" that previous religions, "so-called," had sought to address. This assertion, on the one hand, defines that which has been called "religion" as the effort to respond to such cares and concerns, while, on the other, it at least implicitly raises the question of whether different, more authentic kinds of "religion" might be envisioned. A further and entirely different puzzle, however, is introduced by the next sentence, which states that any attempt to provide a "demonstration" of the thesis that has just been announced can only lead "astray," down the path of a "universal polemic" that would know no limit or measure: *einer maßlosen Universalpolemik*. Taken seriously, this statement suggests how difficult it will be to write a text that does justice to the title "Capitalism as Religion," since any attempt to provide a rigorous demonstration of the thesis suggested by this title is disavowed at the outset. Does this explain why Benjamin left the text unfinished and did not publish it during his lifetime?

Although he does not return to this problem, in his very next sentence Benjamin may provide an implicit commentary on it: "We cannot draw closed the net in which we stand." My rendition of Benjamin's text here departs from the published translation, which reads: "We cannot draw closed the net in which *we are caught*" (288/100). This is surely a more elegant and idiomatic formulation than what I have provided, and yet, as awkward and unusual as my rendering of this sentence may be, it is no less so than Benjamin's German text, which it seeks to reproduce literally. Benjamin indeed describes his situation, and that of his readers, as "standing in a net" rather than being "caught in" one. One does not usually think of oneself, or anything else for that matter, as "standing in a net." And yet that is the position, or posture, Benjamin describes. However awkward and unusual it undoubtedly is, it may help to suggest just what is at stake in the "measureless universal polemics" that any demonstration of his thesis risks unleashing: nothing less than the desire to "take a stand," to achieve a certain stability and steadfastness, all of which is undercut and put into question when that "in" which one seeks to take a "stand" has the character of a "net."

And yet, how does one "stand in a net," given that it consists in strands that comprise a mesh or lattice rather than anything firm or solid? What constitutes a net is utterly relational: more akin to an interval than to a link in a chain. This "intervallic" texture of the net is perhaps the reason why, as Benjamin remarks, it "cannot" be "draw[n] closed." This open, although not borderless, quality of the "net in which we stand" defines the situation in which this text, at any rate, is written. The danger that could trigger those "measureless universal polemics" might thus be related to the risk of losing one's balance, one's "stance," and falling into the meshwork of the net "in which we stand"—or try to, at least. As if to moderate, if not modulate this risk, Benjamin closes his opening paragraph with the promise that "later" we will be able to survey this enigma. Just where or when such an "overview [*Überblick*]" will be possible remains to be seen. But what the risk of a "universal polemic" suggests is that, if capitalism does indeed respond to the same anxieties, torments, and troubles that traditional religions sought to address, the recognition of this affinity is liable to unleash a violence whose effects are difficult to gauge. And this, in turn, would seem to imply that the stability and efficacy of capitalism as a religion depends upon the dissimulation of its religious character.

Having thus introduced his main thesis as well as the problems and risks involved in its demonstration, Benjamin goes on to describe the "three aspects" that render "the religious structure of capitalism recognizable [*erkennbar*]." To these he will later add, as an apparent afterthought, a "fourth" aspect, which, however, will turn out to be the most difficult and decisive of all. But first let us summarize the three initial traits, before going on to discuss them in some detail. "In the first place, capitalism is a purely cultic religion; perhaps the most extreme that has ever existed" (288/100). Second, as a cult-religion, capitalism knows neither pauses nor alternatives, but only a "permanent duration"; as Benjamin puts it, citing a French expression, it is "sans trêve et sans merci," "without truce and without mercy."[4] Third, the mercilessly incessant and indeed warlike nature of capitalism—for without war or some sort of analogous struggle it makes little sense to speak of "truce"—is "presumably the first instance of a cult that culpabilizes rather than atones [*der erste Fall eines nicht entsühnenden, sondern verschuldenden Kultus*]."

Having thus summarized the three initial "traits" through which Benjamin defines capitalism as a religion, we can now take a closer look at them. Although religious, at least in the sense traditionally ascribed to the term, the practice of the capitalist cult does not require a "specific body of dogma" or a "theology." If the essence of a cult as generally understood consists in the worship of some sort of absent or distant entity, in capitalism this entity is determined not through any sort of theological dogma but rather "through an immediate relation to the cult" as such. The replacement of theological dogma by this *immediate* relation to the cult suggests that the religious character of capitalism is inseparable from the celebration of cultic rituals. Whereas capitalism is directed toward something or someone inaccessible, as presumably every cult must be, in capitalism this inaccessibility itself has taken on the character of a certain immediacy. Benjamin refers to "utilitarianism," which, he argues, "from this point of view acquires a religious coloration." The appeal to a transcendent entity associated with traditional religious cults here becomes the appeal to an immanent, if intangible, *quantity*: "the greatest good of the greatest number," a maxim of utilitarianism that Benjamin does not mention. This perspective of quantification, which informs utilitarianism, assumes a "religious" meaning through its relation to the capitalist cult.

Benjamin's elaboration of the two other major traits of the capitalist cult begin to reveal its defining aspects. As a cult, its celebration is marked by *permanence* and *duration*: *permanente Dauer.* This is by no means self-evident with respect to the traditional understanding of a cult, whose ritual practice generally depends upon spatio-temporal limitations. In this sense, the "celebration" of a cult is usually neither of "permanent duration" nor ubiquitous. What distinguishes the capitalist cult, by contrast, is its tendency to unremitting and relentless totalization: "There are no 'weekdays.' There is no day that would not be a festive day [*Festtag*] in the terrible sense of the unfolding of all sacred pomp as well as of the uttermost tension [*Anspan-*

nung]" (288/100). The celebration of the cult may thus be unremitting, but its "permanence" and durability take a toll upon those who practice it: they are subjected to extreme "tension," which presumably leaves them little energy left over for other concerns, including those "cares, torments, troubles" that religions have traditionally sought to assuage. The capitalist cult achieves this effect not through theological dogma but by absorbing and channeling energies into a state of tension that leaves little time or opportunity to worry about anything more remote. It is the *ubiquity* of the *celebration* of the cult that thus supplants transcendence, whether of hope or of despair. It leaves no time for anything else.

This aspect leads to, but also presupposes, the third "trait" of the capitalist cult, its effect of creating guilt: "An enormous consciousness of guilt [*Schuldbewußtein*] that does not know how to atone for itself [*das sich nicht zu entsühnen weiß*] seizes upon the cult, not in order to atone for its guilt but to render it universal" (288/100). The tendency to alleviate the pressure of guilt by universalizing sheds light on the "universal polemics" that would result from any effort to bring the religious nature of capitalism into the open. Universalizing guilt would be a response to the unbearable "tension" produced by guilty conscience—that "enormous consciousness of guilt" lacking any possibility of atonement. In the absence of any alternative to its present situation, the guilty conscience responds by seeking to affirm itself as universal.

This extension does not stop at the borders of the universe. "Above all," Benjamin asserts, capitalism as cult strives to include God Himself in its guilt."[5] Its purpose in so doing is "finally to arouse his interest in atonement," make "despair worldwide," and thus install a situation "which is actually its secret *hope*" (289/101). In other words, the "secret hope" of capitalism as religion and cult resides in the *globalization of despair*, and hence of guilt. Universal guilt, which does not stop short of God Himself, constitutes the secret hope of the capitalist cult insofar as it elevates the isolation of the individual by universalizing it. The concomitant "expansion of despair" into a "religious state of the world at large" produces a situation "from which salvation can be expected."

To be sure, there is a paradox at work in Benjamin's account. The capitalist cult universalizes guilt, extending it to God Himself, and thereby all but eliminating the possibility of atonement. And yet, this inclusion of God in the universe of the guilty is still the bearer of a "secret hope" of salvation. That hope must remain *secret* insofar as the universalization of guilt and despair have all but eliminated any alternative to capitalism. Such a universe leaves no place for anything else, least of all for redemption. All that is conceivable is the continuation of the cult itself. And this is what constitutes the secret *hope* of capitalism: the hope that in the absence of alternatives, it will survive.

But this survival is of a very peculiar kind. The *immediate* effect of the capitalist cult is not so much to worship something or someone that is absent or inaccessible but rather, more crudely, to demolish existence without providing an alternative. In this respect, Benjamin observes:

> Capitalism is entirely without precedent. . . . It is a religion that offers not the reform of existence but its complete destruction. It is the expansion of despair, until despair becomes a worldwide religious state from which salvation can be expected. God's transcendence has fallen. But he is not dead; he has been included in human destiny. This passage of the planet "man" through the house of despair *in the absolute solitude of its path* is the *ethos* that Nietzsche defined. This man is the superman, the first to recognize the religion of capitalism and begin to bring it to fulfillment. (289/101—my emphasis)

The world of capitalism as cult-religion is here situated in the tradition of the Counter-Reformation, which Benjamin will deploy a few years later in his study *The Origin of the German Mourning Play.*[6] The astrological reference to the "passage of the planet 'man' through the house of despair" suggests the return of pagan mythology as part of the crisis of Christian eschatology that Benjamin associates with the Reformation and the responses—above all, "allegory"—it provokes. An essential dimension of this crisis is the isolation of the human individual, no longer firmly situated within the Christian narrative of grace and redemption. This produces what Benjamin, in the passage quoted, describes as "the absolute solitude [*absolute Einsamkeit*]" of the path that leads "the planet 'man' through the house of despair." This absolute solitude and despair of the post-Reformation individual marks both the development of capitalism into a cult-religion and its culmination in the Nietzschean notion of the "superman." The same isolation is also involved in the universalization of guilt without atonement.

Benjamin's reference, in the passage quoted, to the integration of God into "human destiny" must be read in the context of a text he wrote in 1919, which at the time he deemed "one of my best essays"[7]: "Destiny and Character" ("Schicksal und Charakter"). In that text, destiny, which is defined as "the guilt-nexus of the living [*der Schuldzusammenhang des Lebendigen*]," is clearly distinguished from religion: "An order whose sole intrinsic concepts are misfortune and guilt, and within which there is no conceivable path of liberation . . .—such an order cannot be religious, no matter how much the misunderstood concept of guilt appears to suggest the contrary."[8] Developing thoughts that were to come to fruition in his 1921 essay "The Critique of Force," Benjamin distinguishes the sphere of guilt, which he situates in the juridical order of Law and Right,[9] from that of religion, which in this text he associates with liberation. By implication, then, the cult-religion of capitalism functions entirely within the (pagan) juridical order, which it both hypostasizes and universalizes through its extension of guilt to include the Deity Himself. Such an extension is made possible by the twofold determination of human existence as *individual* and *biological*. Seen from the perspective of the isolated individual, mortality is legitimized as the "destiny" or destination of the "guilty." There can be no atoning for a life that is exclusively individual.

This, then, is the paradox raised by the integration of "God's transcendence . . . into the guilt-nexus of the living." Such integration of the Divine can only allow for the hope of redemption if it somehow resists the total immanence that seems to be its "destiny." Perhaps it is this quandary that compels Benjamin to add a fourth trait to his description of the capitalist cult, although he initially had foreseen only three. This fourth feature is introduced immediately following the reference to Nietzsche, and it extends the "secret" to the divine object of the capitalist cult itself: "Its fourth trait is that its God must be kept secret [*verheimlicht*] and only addressed [*angesprochen*] at the zenith of its culpability [*Verschuldung*: also indebtedness]. The cult is celebrated before an unripened [*ungereiften*] deity; each representation, each thought of it violates [*verletzt*] the secret [*Geheimnis*] of its maturity [*Reife*]."[10] The enigma of a deity that must be worshipped by the capitalist cult but at the same time kept *secret*—not just hidden from view, but also inaccessible to thought and representation—is a result of its integration into a human destiny marked by a guilt for which the cult allows no atonement. Any attempt to think or represent this "unripened deity" will necessarily violate "the secret of its maturity." The object of the cult thus has to remain secret because "unripened." Any "hope" based on such a deity can therefore be no less "secret" than the deity itself. Because it is "unripened," this deity can not be represented or thought, but only "addressed," and this "at the zenith of its culpability." By this "address," the deity is "kept secret."

This fourth feature thus entails a deliberate "keeping secret" of the deity worshipped by the capitalist cult, which is linked, on the one hand, to its *Unreife*, immaturity or unripeness, and, on the other, to the culmination of its guilt. Indeed, the very fact that the God is unripe seems to constitute that apogee. The German word *Reife,* like English *ripe*, refers to the life process of maturation. The formerly transcendent divinity, now integrated, or "fallen," into human destiny, is subject to the biological process of growth and decay. This "biologization" of God in the capitalist cult marks the deity as "guilty," since from the point of pure immanence, each living being is, qua individual, deemed "responsible" for its "own" finitude. Insofar as the deity of capitalism is subject to the laws of life construed as immanence, its decay and death is construed as the result of its "guilt." This in turn means that the Deity can survive only insofar as it resists maturation: insofar as it is *and remains* "unripened." Since, however, for all living beings this state is always transitory, it must be "kept secret" if it is to survive as object of the cult. Any "conception" or "representation" of an "unripened" deity—which would have to include that employed by Benjamin himself—would necessarily do violence to the "secret of its ripeness," since this secret can consist only in the unthinkable, unrepresentable duration of its "unripeness": in the maximization of its "shelf-life," one might say today.

What the cult of capitalism cultivates is the secret of this unripeness. Since the deity thus addressed is in contradiction with itself, it can be said to be addressed "at the zenith of its culpability." The Nietzschean "thought" of the superman both recognizes yet also mystifies the unthinkably secret guilt of this "address," according to Benjamin: "The thought of the *Übermensch* transposes the apocalyptic 'leap' [*Sprung*] not into reversal [*Umkehr*], atonement [*Sühne*], purification, penance [*Büsse*], but rather into ostensibly continuous, although ultimately explosive, discontinuous elevation [*Steigerung*]. . . . The *superman* is the historical man who without reversal [*ohne Umkehr*] has reached the sky and *outgrown* it" (289/101).

The "apocalyptic leap" implied in the Nietzschean notion of the superman is thus divested of a radical discontinuity to which Benjamin here gives different names—above all, *Umkehr*, "reversal," and *Sühne*, "atonement." Instead of discontinuity and the alterity it entails, the superman embodies the quantitative intensification and elevation of a "historical man" who is no longer subject to the categorical change of course implied in the notion of *Umkehr*. This term recalls Hölderlin's use in his notion of a *vaterländische Umkehr*, a "patriotic overturning," which in his "Notes on Sophocles' *Antigone*" he defines as "the overturning of all forms and modes of representation," immediately adding that "such an utter overturning in this sense . . . just as an utter overturning in general, without anything to hold onto [*ohne allen Halt*] is not permitted man as a cognitive being."[11] As Heidegger will do in his lectures on Nietzsche and Hölderlin some fifteen years later, Benjamin contrasts Nietzsche, as the thinker who consummates a certain religious-metaphysical tradition—albeit negatively, by envisaging its demolition [*Zertrümmerung*]—with Hölderlin, whose notion of *Umkehr* implies a break with that tradition and the beginning of something radically different. Yet if we pay close attention to Benjamin's text, we see that this contrast consists, not in a clear-cut opposition between the two thinkers, but in a demarcation of their respective projects. For Benjamin, Nietzsche's notion of the superman (or overman) "is the first to begin to fulfill the capitalist religion *cognitively* [erkennend]." Despite his constant critique of knowledge, Nietzsche, for Benjamin at least, is still bent on producing new knowledge. Hölderlin, by contrast, though Benjamin does not explicitly cite him here, insists that his notion of "patriotic overturning" must remain inaccessible to man insofar as he is a *cognitive being*. The Hölderlinian notion of *Umkehr* is not, therefore, accessible to a primarily cognitive discourse, but rather to one that is poetic.

If, then, capitalism as religious cult is to be thought in terms of its possibilities of *Umkehr*, in the Hölderlinian sense, at least, it must be approached from a perspective that does not merely treat it as an object of knowledge. As such an object, it will be understood only in terms of a "continuous intensification or elevation [*kontinuierliche Steigerung*]," and thus its intrinsic discontinuities will be misconstrued. In this sense, the destructive force of the Nietzschean superman, anticipating a moment when "the heavens will explode through heightened humanity [*gesteigerte Menschlichkeit*]," prolongs a historical tradition marked by "religious culpabilization [*religiöse Verschuldung*]," but does not open the perspective of a future that would be essentially different.

Benjamin also applies this model of the critic who continues and consummates the cult of capitalism to Freud and Marx: he describes repression as a kind of capital that bears interest in the "hell of the unconscious," and he portrays socialism, no less briefly and schematically, as resulting from the "interest and compound interest that are functions of *Schuld*," but that serve to maintain the essence of a "capitalism that is not being overturned [*der nicht umkehrende Kapitalismus*]." It is of at least passing interest that Benjamin here invokes the interest-bearing function of money as the salient trait of the capitalist cult-religion, rather than the exploitation of social labor, which for Marx, at least, is the decisive factor in the production of surplus-value. Benjamin, in short, places money rather than labor at the heart of his discussion of "capitalism as religion." Money appears as the form in which, or rather the stage upon which, the secret and unripe deity worshipped by the capitalist cult takes its hidden place. And Benjamin evokes money as that which defines the historical relation of capitalist cult-religion to its religious predecessors:

> Capitalism—as could be shown not just with Calvinism, but with the other orthodox Christian tendencies—developed in the West parasitically out of Christianity, the history of which in the end [*zuletzt*] and in essence is that of a parasite, capitalism. . . . The Christianity of the Reformation period did not simply favor the emergence of capitalism—it transformed itself into capitalism.
>
> Comparison between the pictures of saints in different religions, on the one hand, and the banknotes of different states on the other. The spirit that speaks out of the ornaments on banknotes. (289–90/102)

The parasitic relation of capitalism to Christianity is here described as a transformation of what Schmitt designates as the "principle of representation." This transformation is articulated in the shift from the depictions of saints to the ornamentality that characterizes the banknotes of different national currencies. Like Schmitt, in short, Benjamin sees nation-states as heirs to the different Christian churches. But unlike Schmitt, Benjamin emphasizes that "the spirit"—*der Geist*—common to both traditional religion and capitalist nation-states manifests itself in different ways in each. In the secular world of nation-states, and above all of their financial institutions, this spirit no longer requires direct human representations—representation of "persons," as Schmitt would insist—in order to "speak." Instead, it speaks "out of ornaments," so long as those ornaments are used to distinguish monetary units from one another. In short, quantitative monetary distinctions acquire a voice, but not necessarily a face: their abstractness is more appropriately expressed by "ornaments" than by human forms or figures.

With the comparison between the pictures of saints and the ornaments on banknotes, the structure and syntax of this text change. Discursive continuity is replaced by a more fragmentary, telegraphic style of notation, as though Benjamin were jotting down suggestions for further study rather than elaborating a coherent argument. This becomes unmistakable a few lines further on, when he returns to the question of the historical relation of capitalism to Christianity:

> Christianity during the time of the Reformation did not facilitate the rise of capitalism but rather transformed itself into capitalism.
>
> Methodically one should begin by investigating the different connections with myth that money entered into in the course of its history, until it had extracted so many mythical elements from Christianity that it could establish its own myth. . . . Pluto as the god of wealth. (290/102)

If one reads these lines as in part an anticipation of the analysis of Reformation and Counter-Reformation Christianity that Benjamin would begin to elaborate shortly after writing this essay and that he would publish in his book on the German mourning play, one can provide the following interpretation: Capitalism emerges as the most successful effort of the Counter-Reformation to meet the challenge of Luther's "storm against the work," which is to say, against the ability of institutionalized religion to provide a consoling response to the "cares, torments, troubles" that crystallize around anxieties of mortality. With Luther's doctrine of *sola fides,* "faith alone" as the path to salvation, the continuum of representation embodied in the Church, its rites and sacraments, is no longer uncontested. In its place, the isolated individual emerges as the locus of the "faith" that "alone" has saving power. The separation of faith from dogmatic theology, but also from the phenomenal world—since it is situated "within" the individual—renders mediation, traditionally performed by Church ritual and sacraments, problematic. Schmitt's principle of representation is challenged, if not supplanted, by what Benjamin, in *The Origin of the German Mourning Play*, describes as "the antinomies of the allegorical," which both elevate and degrade everything represented by subjecting it to the uncertainties of an undemonstrable faith.

Paradoxically, perhaps, the undemonstrability of this "faith alone," cut off from "good works," opens up a new role for "knowledge." If the aim of the capitalist cult is, as Benjamin writes, "to hold out until the end" (289/103), then this aim can only be attained by a knowledge that fulfills the previous function of dogmatic theology while no longer depending upon it. Such knowledge must acknowledge the ambivalence of a phenomenal world without good works, without, however, replacing them with access to a pure and simple transcendence. And yet, this knowledge has as its imperative task to invest the "end" with a new meaning in the world of immanence of capitalist cult-religion. This is perhaps why, in a series of cryptic notes toward the end of the fragment, Benjamin suddenly turns to a particular kind of knowledge: "Connection between the dogma of the destructive [*auflösenden*]—but for us both redeeming and lethal [*uns in dieser Eigenschaft zugleich erlösenden und tötenden*] nature of knowledge, and capitalism: the *bottom line* [*die Bilanz*] as the knowledge that both redeems and eliminates [*als das erlösende und erledigende Wissen*]" (290/103, my emphasis). The "spirit" that speaks out of the ornaments on the banknotes *speaks to* the knowledge of the *bottom line*. By translating all phenomena into the quantitative relation of the bottom line, it "destroys" their qualitative specificity, "kills" their immediate self-presence, yet at the same time "redeems" them as (commodity) value. From the point of view of traditional "dogma," such knowledge is seen as strictly destructive, "dissolving" the "natural" connections of phenomena with the world. But "for us," Benjamin writes—that is, for those who must stand "in the net"—it is "both redeeming and lethal."

The root, in German, of two of the three words used by Benjamin to describe the nature of knowledge—*auflösend* and *erlösend*—is *lösen*. It suggests a loosening of ties, links, and connections, the experience of which runs the gamut of extremes between processes of disintegration and separation, on the one hand, and those of resolution and redemption, on the other. In the context in which Benjamin places it, however, the major effect of this new knowledge is to replace the phenomenal world of things with the "balance sheet" and its "bottom line" (the word he uses, *Bilanz*, signifies both). The *Bilanz* installs commercial calculation as the model of knowledge, which in turn serves to link the invisible "faith" of the individual to the phenomenal world of capitalism. It is possible, indeed inevitable, to "hold out until the end" once that "end" is determined as the bottom line, for each bottom line ends one balance sheet and begins another. The process is in principle infinite and yet immanent.

This knowledge of the bottom line reconciles not just the books, which must balance, but also what Benjamin, without referring to Nietzsche, calls the "demonic ambiguity of *Schuld*," as both moral culpability and indebtedness. *Schuld* thus becomes "redeemable" and time calculable in the fortunate fall down to the bottom line. The bottom line thus is the hidden deity worshipped by the capitalist cult: always "unripe" because ever renewable, it is the always opportune "target of opportunity" of a knowledge and a practice that kill in order to redeem.

The Target in the Carpet

Death thus emerges as the price of redemption. As such, it becomes meaningful and even legitimate. But to do so, it must be the object of will and intention. This is what knowledge of the bottom line accomplishes: It kills in order to redeem. The cult of capitalism thus produces and reproduces guilt—*Schuld*—which it redeems, but for which it does not atone. There is no atonement precisely because of redemption: The redemption of *Schuld* is inseparable from its reproduction; each bottom line is a new limit to be exceeded. The god that is worshipped remains forever "unripened," but its *telos* remains that of a ripening without end. The pursuit of this end without end through countless bottom lines does not eliminate the "cares" and concerns—*Sorgen*—mentioned at the outset of the essay: it only increases them.

> "Cares": a spiritual malady peculiar to the capitalist period. . . . A condition that leaves no way out [*Ausweg*] produces guilt. "Cares" are the index of this guilty conscience of the blind alley. "Cares" emerge in the anxiety of a blind alley that is communal [*gemeinschaftsmäßig*], not individual. (290/102)

Benjamin's note here seems to anticipate the analysis of *Schuld* and *Sorge* that Heidegger will later elaborate in *To Be and Time* (*Sein und Zeit*), but it does so with two important distinctions. First, Benjamin's point of departure is not the trans-historical being of "everyday," but rather the "capitalist period." Second, and even more important, it is the celebration of the capitalist cult, and the redemptive *Schuld* it produces, that is responsible for the sense of despair, the *Sorge*, that marks the capitalist era. The content of this *Sorge* is twofold and ambiguous. On the one hand, it is a response to the lack of alternatives or, more precisely, the lack of an *exit*, of a *way out* of the immanence of the capitalist cult and its succession of balance sheets. On the other, as "care" and "concern" it is irreducibly *communal*, and as such seeks an alternative to the individualist straitjacket of the capitalist cult-religion. But celebration of the cult, which aspires to be total and global, seeks to bar all such alternatives.

"Later, however, an overview will be possible." We are, to be sure, still waiting for that "later." It may be a long wait. Benjamin himself never finished or returned to this initial elaboration of "capitalism as religion." But in an even earlier text, which he designated his "first major work," he approached some of the same questions in a way that could possibly point, if not to a "way out," at least to a different kind of response to the "cares, torments, troubles to which in the past the so-called religions offered answers." This essay, written shortly after the outbreak of the First World War, consists in a reading of two poems by Hölderlin, "Poetic Courage" ("Dichtermut") and "Timidity" ("Blödigkeit").[12] The text was composed after the suicide of his close friend, the poet Fritz Heinle. It is hardly surprising, therefore, that one of the major motifs the essay addresses, through its reading of Hölderlin, concerns the relation of the poet—as one of the "living"—to death. Benjamin begins this text by distinguishing between the poem (*das Gedicht*) and what he calls "the poeticized [*das Gedichtete*]."[13] He defines this notion of the "poetic" as a "liminal concept [*Grenzbegriff*]" with respect to the poem, from which it distinguishes itself "strictly through its greater determinability [*größere Bestimmbarkeit*]."[14] At the same time, Benjamin acknowledges that this "greater determinability," far from exhausting the poem as a whole, is achieved only "by disregarding certain [of its] determinations." In short, the "possibility" of determining the poem as "the poeticized" is never simply a realization or actualization of the poem as such, in its entirety or essence, but rather a *selection*, which is always partial, if not partisan. The "poeticized" thus has to do with *relations*, rather than with substances—or, as Benjamin calls it in this essay—with the *functional unity* that characterizes the poem as a work. The relational network that constitutes "the poeticized" is not, therefore, limited to the poem as such, but rather consists in "the potential existence of determinations," including those "that are . . . actualized in the poem *and others*" (20/106). In short, the relations that constitute "the poeticized" do not have to be actually present or explicit in the poem, but can entail its implicit ramifications. This corresponds to the "liminal" position of "the poeticized," which Benjamin defines as situated between the poem and life: it marks "the transition from the functional unity of life to that of the poem." This "transition" Benjamin also describes as a "task [*Aufgabe*]," which derives from "the solution that is the poem" (19/107). In other words, the poem is defined as the solution to the task that has to be formulated *post facto* as the poeticized. It is this quality of the poeticized as task, Benjamin argues, which makes "an evaluation [*Beurteilung*] of the poem possible" (19/107). Interpretation thus does not judge the poem directly but rather reconstructs, as the poeticized, the task accomplished by and as the poem.

Significantly, the immediate object and result of Benjamin's reading, "the poeticized," has a different structure from that of the two poles between which it is situated, life and the poem. The latter he designates as a "functional unity [*Funktionseinheit*]," whereas he describes the former as a "manifold of connections [*Mannigfaltigkeit der Verbindungen*]." The Kantian resonances of this term are heightened when Benjamin defines this "manifold" as the "a priori of the poem," insofar as it determines its relation to "life." At the same time, this same "manifold of connections" renders the poeticized unattainable in its purity: "The disclosure of the pure poeticized, of the absolute task, must, after all that has been said, remain a purely methodological, ideal goal" (21/108).

The poeticized thus presents the ideal target of knowledge, one, however, that as such remains inaccessible to it. Benjamin thus elaborates a notion of interpretation in which the target—the goal—remains unattainable, and only as such determining. The *concept* of "connection"—*Verbindung*—which is an essential condition of the determinability of the poetic, is itself determined through its irreducible *connection to the "disregard" presupposed by that very same "determinability."* In short, connections can be made only by unmaking others. Targets can be "hit" only by at the same time missing something else that is not merely external to the target but belongs to it—or, rather, to which the target itself belongs.

We need to keep the paradoxical quality of these "connections" in mind, since the term will recur as a motif in Benjamin's reading of the two poems. Although an exhaustive discussion of this reading is not possible here—nor perhaps elsewhere, for the very reasons just discussed—I will try to sketch some of its major traits and contours.

The motif common to both poems, according to Benjamin, is the "death of the poet." But it is articulated very differently in each. The first poem, "Poetic Courage," he describes as marked by "considerable indeterminacy of the visual [*des Anschaulichen*] and by a lack of connection in its individual [elements] [*Unverbundenheit im einzelnen*]." The connections made in the poem—for instance, concerning the relation of mortal and divine existence—remain abstract and are established strictly through recourse to Greek mythology:

> The myth emerges here out of mythology. The sun god is the poet's antecedent and his dying is the destiny through which the poet's death, at first mirrored, becomes real. . . . The same indeterminacy of the formative principle, which demarcates itself so sharply from the Greece that is conjured up, threatens the entire poem. . . . The relation of gods and men to the poetic world, to the spatio-temporal unity in which they live, is organized neither intensively nor in a purely Greek manner. . . . The connectedness [*Verbundenheit*] of the God with humans is constrained by rigid rhythms into one great image. But in its isolation it is unable to interpret the basis of those connected powers [*den Grund jener verbundenen Mächte*] and loses itself. . . . The poetic law has not yet saturated this Hölderlinian world. (23–24/111)

Such critical remarks suggest, by negation, what might be understood positively under "the poetic law [*das dichterische Gesetz*]" but is not yet realized in "Poetic Courage." Shortly following the quoted passage, Benjamin describes the positive alternative that will be implemented in the second poem he will discuss, "Timidity." He designates its principle as the "law of identity": "The law of identity states that all unities in the poem appear already in intensive interpenetration; that the elements are never purely graspable, that, rather, one can grasp only *the structure of their relations* [*das Gefüge ihrer Beziehungen*], in which individual identity is a *function of an infinite chain or series*, in which the poeticized unfolds" (112/25, my emphasis). Through this definition of "individual identity" as a "function of an infinite chain or series," the individual is inscribed or situated in a chain that is infinite—or, as Freud formulates it in *The Man Moses*, a chain that "cannot be traced any further."[15] What begins to emerge is another kind of "knowledge," which would not be fixed or focused upon the "bottom line" of the "balance sheet" but rather would take (its) place in a chain without knowable beginning or end. This law of identity, as

Benjamin describes it, is itself the function of a certain kind of "balancing" act, but one that does not produce an equilibrium, much less a bottom line:

> Here, at the center of the poem, the orders of gods and men are curiously raised up toward and against each other, the one balanced by the other. (Like two scales: they are left in their opposing positions, yet lifted off the scale beam. From this emerges, very graphically, the fundamental formal law of the *poeticized*, the origin of that order of law whose realization gives the later version [i.e., "Timidity"] its foundation. . . . This is the law of identity—the law according to which all essences in the *poeticized* are revealed as the unity of what are in principle infinite functions. No element can ever be singled out, void of relation, from the intensity of the world order, which is fundamentally felt. (25/112)

This sort of knowledge, which, as we have just read, must be "felt" no less than thought, Benjamin designates as "being-known"—*Bekannt-Sein*—and precisely its "being," which, unlike traditional knowledge, is not directed at an isolated object but rather is involved in an infinite network, entails a different relation to life on the part of the "living," *den Lebendigen*:

> In this world of Hölderlin, the living are always clearly the stretching *[Erstreckung]* of space, the spread-out plane, in which (as will become visible) destiny extends itself [*sich . . . erstreckt*]. Much, very much is said about Hölderlin's cosmos in the words that follow, which—strange once again, as though from the world of the East, and yet how much more originary than the Greek Parca—confer majesty upon the poet: "Does your foot not stride on the true as upon carpets?" [*Geht auf Wahrem dein Fuß nicht, wie auf Teppichen?*] (26/114)

These passages suggest a conception of the "living" very different from what is usually associated with the word—a conception determined by its position, or, as we shall soon see, its "layout." In this layout, figures such as *chain* and *net* will play determining roles. Far from construing human life in terms of self-standing immanence or interiority, Benjamin here thinks "the living" in the plural and in regard to a certain dispersion or "stretching." Thus, whereas the author of "Capitalism as Religion" begins by determining his position and that of his readers as one of "standing in" a "net," the Hölderlinian poem, at least as "poeticized" by Benjamin, asks about a certain "striding," "walking," or "going": "Geht auf Wahrem dein Fuß nicht, wie auf Teppichen?" Instead of the *assertion* of a paradoxical "stance," there is the *question* of a poet's "foot" striding on "the true" as though on "carpets." Instead of stability, there is a movement between the singularity of "the true" and the plurality of "carpets."

Such a movement is determined by what Benjamin calls "the truth of the layout [Die Wahrheit der Lage], which, as the ordering concept of the Hölderlinian world, is necessarily presupposed [by the image]" (26/114). This "spatial principle" of the layout—which offers a radical alternative to Schmitt's "representation principle"—makes possible another conception of identity, which emerges out of the interaction of "layout [*Lage*]" and that which is "opportunely *laid*-out [*Gelegenem*]," or, to put it more concisely, the interaction of *situation* and *situatedness*:

> Space is to be grasped as the identity of layout and laid-out [*Lage* and *Gelegenem*]. Immanent to everything determining in space is its own determination. Every layout is determined solely in space and in it alone determining. Just as the image of the carpet (since a plane is laid down here as the foundation of an intellectual system) should recall its exemplary pattern [*Musterhaftigkeit*], rendering visible the intellectual arbitrariness of the ornament—and since the ornament constitutes a true determination of the layout, rendering it absolute—so the traversable [*beschreitbaren*] order of truth itself entails *the intensive activity of the gait as its inner, plastic temporal form.* This intellectual region is traversable [*beschreitbar*], and with every step the strider remains necessarily in the realm of the true. . . .

> *The temporal form in the unending stretching, the truth of the layout*, binds the living to the poet. (27/115, my emphasis)

Thus understood, identity consists in the reciprocal determination of layout and laid-out, *Lage* and *Gelegenem*, which in their interaction produce an exemplary pattern, a *Muster*. This pattern, although exemplary, is not representational but "arbitrary," hence determined not through its content but through its context: its spatial disposition, its layout. The determining layout, however, is not only spatial, but also temporal. Such spatio-temporal determination is what Benjamin, following Hölderlin, calls "*Gelegenheit*," normally translated "opportunity," but literally "laid out or down" at a certain moment in time. This moment of opportunity, however, is one not to be "seized," but traversed: it is a "port" or "portal" (lexical root of "op*port*unity"), which leads not to an ultimate goal but to a multitude of "carpets." These carpets are, paradoxically, both singular and plural, "singularly plural," as Jean-Luc Nancy might put it,[16] neither infinite nor simply finite. In striding on them, the poet does not seek to reach a goal or hit a target, nor does he attempt to draw them to a close or into a unity, but instead allows his footsteps to be drawn into them, knowing that, wherever they fall, those steps will always "remain in the realm of the true."

The plurality of the carpets belongs to a "realm of the true" that is always irreducibly singular. The German word *Raum*, somewhat like English *room*, articulates this notion of singular plurality, negotiating between "space" and "place." This sort of "room" or *Raum* is the site of the "ornament," which in its exemplary patterning, its *Musterhaftigkeit, signifies* but does not *represent*. An ornament can never claim to be self-contained. Rather, it demands to be seen as the result of a movement that is inseparable from a singular and mortal body, from a "foot" that "strides" but that must "remain in the true." This singularity finds expression in a verse of the poem Benjamin cites: "Whatever happens, let it all be laid out opportunely for you [*Was geschieht, es sei alles gelegen dir*]." The addressee ("you") is summoned, not to *seize* the opportunity as a means to an end, but to *respond* to it as a layout that demands to be traversed, explored, but never transcended. Part of the singular nature of the true is to be laid out in many carpets, in multiple opportunities, laid down in different ways, which, however plural, remain always singular. "The true," as distinct from "truth," is inseparable from a relation that is *irreducibly singular*; as an adjectival-adverbial noun, it designates a *way of being* that is dependent on its situation rather than anything like an intrinsic content or quality. It will therefore vary from situation to situation, from *Lage* to *Lage*, thus requiring an articulation that leaves room for such variability. This leads Benjamin to introduce a concept with a strong Nietzschean resonance: "imagistic dissonance [*Bilddissonanz*]."[17]

> Thus, the imagistic dissonance of the true and the carpet calls up *stridability* [*Beschreitbarkeit*] as the relation that unifies the [conflicting] orders, just as "opportunity laid out" [*Gelegenheit*] determines the intellectual-temporal identity (the truth) of the layout [*der Lage*]. The bearers of this relation are predominantly and clearly the living. A path and skillfully sent goal [*Eine Bahn und schickliches Ziel*] must now, precisely in view of the imagistic extremes, appear in an utterly different light.

Only by singularizing itself as the (opportunely) laid out does the layout deploy its truth as that of always singular situations and irreducibly dissonant images. A decade later, Benjamin will discover a similar phenomenon in "the antinomies of the allegorical," which become predominant in the German seventeenth-century mourning play.[18]

Benjamin's phrase "a path and skillfully sent goal" refers to the last strophe of "Timidity," in which the mission of the poet is described: "Good also are, and skillfully sent to someone for something, we [*Gut auch sind und geschickt einem zu etwas wir*]." Here Benjamin sees the double determination of the poet: sent (*geschickt*) to fulfill a task that he "skillfully [*geschickt*]" can accomplish. But the content and addressee of the goal are left strangely vague: "einem zu etwas wir," literally, "to someone for something we." The "we" comes at the end. All that is fixed is the singular nature of both the "someone" and the "something" that constitute the mission. Out of this Benjamin reads what is perhaps the most singular and significant dimension of the poem: "The middle of this world is due another [*gebührt einem anderen*]. . . . For the ultimate law of this world is the obligation of being connected [*die Verbundenheit*]: as the functional unity of connecting and connected [*von Verbindenden und Verbundenem*]" (32/122). The obligation that thus constitutes "the last law of this world" is designated by Benjamin with the overdetermined German word *Verbundenheit*. It signifies both a state of being "obligated" and, more familiarly, "connectedness." Such connectedness obliges, but differently from the "guilt" of the capitalist cult or of its religious antecedents. This obligation does not promise to make the poets or the living into Gods, nor does it hold out the hope of personal immortality. On the contrary, it exhorts the poet "to step naked into life [*bar ins Leben*]" "and have no care [*und sorge nicht*]." The "step into life" is "bare," stripped of all guarantees, defenses, and security systems—above all, of the ostensibly protective practice of targeting. The admonition to step "bare into life" urges engagement with a world whose center "is due to another" and not to the self. This other can only be identified with the poet insofar as "the principle of the poeticized is above all the exclusive dominion of relation [*Alleinherrschaft der Beziehung*]" (34/124). Relation that rules "exclusively" excludes every possibility of being subordinated to a constitutive subject, either as a self or as self-consciousness, and this holds for the poet no less than for capital.

To be sure, Benjamin, mourning the self-inflicted death of his poet-friend, on the eve of the death of millions of others, who were neither poets nor friends—seeks to give his reading of the two Hölderlin poems a consoling conclusion, in which "infinite figure and lack of figuration, temporal sculpture and spatial existence, idea and sensibility" are in the end harmoniously united. But such union no longer respects the *exclusive* rule of *relation* in the poeticized. It thus may be necessary to re-poeticize Benjamin's text just as he did Hölderlin's, reading it "through the potential existence of determinations present in the text'' that point to others, existing virtually *elsewhere* (20/106). A ''critical'' text need be no more a unity than ''the poeticized,'' *das Gedichtete*. But when we thus *part with* the text, we remain in contact with it. We must, literally, not just depart *from* it, but part *with* it: *stay with* it even in departing *from* it.

In so doing, we follow a hint contained in the following brief remark, made shortly before the end of the essay: ''The consideration of the poeticized however leads not to myth, but rather—in great creations—only to mythic connections and obligations [*nur auf die mythischen Verbundenheiten*]'' (35/126). These connections-obligations cease to be myths or mythological insofar as they produce stories that are recounted, listened to, retold, and transmitted, and in so doing ''produce the net that all stories form with each other *in the end*.'' This *end*, however, will never be present as such, not, at least, as a conclusive conclusion or as the bottom line of a balance sheet, but, rather, only as another singular interruption in an ongoing scansion. It is perhaps not excessive to suggest that such scansions and interruptions constitute the rhythm of what has been called ''tradition.'' Its great chance is that, in remaining unfinished, it keeps itself open to a future that no target practice will ever exhaust.

Notes

Preface

1. "Lesser Hippias," trans. Benjamin Jowett, in *Plato: The Collected Dialogues* (New York: Pantheon Books, 1961), 213.

1. "A Rather Singular Strike"

1. Barton Gellmann and Dana Priest, " 'Target of Opportunity' Seized," *Washington Post*, March 20, 2003.

2. According to recent revelations made by Richard A. Clark, head of counterterrorism at the time, and supported by his former deputy, Roger Cressey, already on the night of September 12, 2001, President Bush insisted that Clark see "if Saddam is linked to this in any way," ignoring Clark's protest that "the culprit was Al Qaeda, not Iraq" ("Ex Bush Aide Finding Fault Sets Off Debate," *New York Times, March 23, 2004,* p. 1).

3. R. A. Hewitt, "Target of Opportunity: Tales and Contrails of the Second World War," MS., 2000.

4. Jean-Luc Nancy, "Dies Irae," in Jacques Derrida et al., *La Faculté de juger* (Paris: Minuit, 1980), 41; unless otherwise specified, this and all other translations are my own.

5. "Ends are sovereign qua ends, which is to say qua tasks" (ibid., 40 n.).

6. In an effort to get closer to the Greek text, I have drawn on a number of existing translations, including those by E.V. Rieu (Baltimore: Penguin, 1946) and W. H. D. Rouse (1937; rpt. New York: The New American Library, 1999), as well as the German translation by Wolfgang Schadewaldt (Hamburg: Rowohlt, 1958).

7. The close relationship between competitive sporting events and violence is found in the Greek myth of the origin of the Olympiad. According to one legend, in the ninth century BC, a period of internecine conflict in Greece, the Delphic Oracle advised Iphitos, king of the small Greek state Elides, where Olympus is situated, to reestablish the competitive games, which were supposed to have existed in the fourteenth century BC, in homage to the gods. Lycurgus, King of Sparta, recognized Elides as a neutral state. These two cities, as well as other participating states, agreed to lay down their arms for the duration of the games, which were known as the Olympiades. Gregory Nagy links such festivals of competitive sporting events—in particular, the race—to the "death of the hero." (*Pindar's Homer: The Lyric Possession of an Epic Past* [Baltimore: The Johns Hopkins University Press, 1980], chap. 4).

8. Stephen Halliwell, *Aristotle's Poetics* (Chicago: University of Chicago Press, 1993), 216.

9. Ibid., 230.

10. This determination of *tuchē* as a causality beyond human comprehension anticipates Kant's move in introducing his notion of "reflective judgment" as involving the counterfactual hypothesis of an "understanding like our own" that is supposed to have produced the singular "form" that "our" understanding cannot apprehend as such. See Immanuel Kant, *Critique of Judgment*, Introduction, IV.

11. H.-P. Stahl, *Thucydides: Man's Place in History* (Llandysul, Ceredigion, Wales: The Classical Press of Wales, 2003), 52.

2. "The Principle of Representation": Carl Schmitt's *Roman Catholicism and Political Form*

1. My translation of the German version by Friedrich Hölderlin, *Sämtliche Werke* (Basel: Stroemfeld/Roter Stern, 1988), 245.

2. Jacques Derrida, *Aporias*, trans. Thomas Dutoit (Stanford: Stanford University Press, 1993), 43.

3. Ibid., 22.

4. Carl Schmitt, *Römische Katholizismus und Politische Form* (Stuttgart: Klett, 1984), 5; *Roman Catholicism and Political Form*, trans. G. L. Ulman (Westport, Ct.: Greenwood Press, 1996), 3. Future references to this work will be given in the text, with both German and English page numbers, although all translations are my own. German page numbers will precede English page numbers.

5. Manfred Dahlheimer, *Der deutsche Katholizismus, 1888–1936* (Paderborn: Ferdinand Schöningh, 1999), 111. Cited in Gopal Balakrishnan, *The Enemy: An Intellectual Portrait of Carl Schmitt* (London: Verso, 2000), 274–75.

6. Carl Schmitt, *Politische Theologie*, (Berlin: Duncker & Humboldt, 1985), 69.

7. *Das Grosse Wörterbuch der deutschen Sprache*, 2d ed., vol. 6 (Mannheim: Duden, 1994), 2761.

8. According to the OED, however, the English word *representation* once had some of the connotations that are still alive in German, including that of theatrical performance.

9. In an early essay, *Gesetz und Urteil*, 2d ed. (Munich: C. H. Beck, 1969), Schmitt argues that a judicial verdict cannot be derived from a norm and hence should not be understood as a mode of "judgment." Note that the German word *Urteil* is used to designate both a logical judgment and a judicial verdict. Schmitt begins by criticizing precisely that conflation. This non-normative character makes the verdict (*Urteil*) a *decision* rather than anything like a logical judgment. Kant struggles with a similar problem in his Introduction to the *Critique of Judgment*, but attempts to save the notion of "judgment" by distinguishing between "determining" judgments, which have objective validity, and "reflecting" judgments, which are merely subjective and heuristic. (See Immanuel Kant, *Critique of Judgment*, Introduction, IV). Schmitt shares with the Kant of the third *Critique* the conviction that established concepts can never exhaustively anticipate or subsume possible experience (which he equates with "nature") and that therefore the problem of "judging" in the absence of applicable general rules is one that his critical philosophy cannot leave unresolved. Schmitt's notion of "decision" may thus be situated within the continuity of this Kantian problematic, especially in its subjectivist aspect.

10. Schmitt, *Politische Theologie*, 41–42.

11. Ibid., 42.

12. The media strategy of Pope John Paul II, displaying to the world his slow but steady physical decline over the past decade, seems to follow a similar line of thought—and belief. Throughout his essay Schmitt emphasizes the importance Catholicism attaches to the "public" sphere, in contrast to the valorization of the private he takes to be characteristic of Protestantism.

13. After two hours dedicated almost exclusively to depicting the death of Christ as the result of savage, sadistic violence, Mel Gibson's film *The Passion of the Christ* does not fail to conclude with a brief

vision of the resurrection of the body, healed of all its mutilations except for the stigmata, as reminder of the redemptive force of representation. The image of the Resurrection serves as the happy ending of a narrative that would otherwise simply add a particularly gruesome chapter to the history of martyrdom—a history that not only shows not the slightest sign of ending, happily or otherwise, but that, conversely, has increased exponentially in past decades, changing the nature of political conflict and, indeed, of conflict tout court.

14. Carl Schmitt, *Verfassungslehre (*Berlin: 1983), 210.

3. Wartime: Freud's "Timely Thoughts on War and Death"

1. Friedrich Nietzsche, *Kritische Gesamtausgabe*, 3.1 (1872–1874), ed. G. Colli and M. Montinari (Berlin: Walter de Gruyter, 1971), 242. Future references will appear in the text.

2. This text by Freud was published in English under the title "Thoughts for the Times on War and Death, "*The Standard Edition of the Complete Psychological Works of Sigmund Freud*, ed. James Strachey (London: Hogarth, 1953–74), 14:273–300. Page references to the German edition—"Zeitgemäßes über Krieg und Tod," *Gesammelte Werke* (Frankfurt a. M.: S. Fischer, 1968), 10:324–55 (hereafter *GW*)—will be given in the body of the text.

3. "Most decisive, however, is rhetoric in the sense of what one might call representative discourse, rather than discussion or debate. It moves in antitheses. But these are not contradictions; they are the various and sundry elements moulded into a *complexio* and thus give life to discourse. . . . All this presupposes a hierarchy, because the spiritual resonance of great rhetoric derives from the belief in the representation claimed by the orator" (Carl Schmitt, *Roman Catholicism and Political Form*, trans. G. L. Ulmen [Westport, Ct.: Greenwood Press, 1966], 23–24).

4. Letter of December 28, 1914, cited in Ernest Jones, *The Life and Work of Sigmund Freud*, (London: Hogarth Press, 1967), 2:413.

5. Sigmund Freud, "Triebe und Triebschicksale," *GW*, 10:214–15.

6. Carl Schmitt, *Der Begriff des Politischen*, 34, n.10.

7. In our own times, the spread of AIDS and the mortality associated with it have had a similar effect.

8. Jacques Derrida, *Specters of Marx: The State of the Debt, the Work of Mourning, and the New International*, trans. Peggy Kamuf (New York: Routledge, 1994), 193.

9. Sigmund Freud, "Die Verneinung," *GW*, 14:12.

10. For the ramifications of such a "network," see chapters 4–6 of this book.

11. Sigmund Freud, "Hemmung, Symptom und Angst," *GW*, 14:151.

12. "The living ego is auto-immune. . . . To protect its life, to constitute itself as a living ego, to relate, as the same, to itself, it is necessarily led to welcome the other within . . . it must therefore take the immune defenses apparently meant for the non-ego, the enemy, the opposite, the adversary *and direct them at once for itself and against itself*" (Derrida, *Specters of Marx*, 140, my italics; see also Jacques Derrida, "Faith and Knowledge," trans. S. Weber, in Jacques Derrida and Gianni Vattimo, eds., *Religion* [Stanford: Stanford University Press, 1998], 40, p. 51).

4. Doing Away with Freud's *Man Moses*

1. Jacques Derrida, *Without Alibi*, trans. Peggy Kamuf (Stanford: Stanford University Press, 2002), 238–80. Further page numbers will be given in the text.

2. Precisely because there can be little doubt about the link between pleasure and suffering or making one suffer, to write of "suffering *just to suffer*" can easily be misunderstood. If suffering and, even more, making suffer can be a source of pleasure, as in sadomasochism, then it is not just suffering for the sake of suffering. This question defines the horizon of the following remarks.

3. Sigmund Freud, *Moses and Monotheism*, trans. Katherine Jones (New York: Vintage, 1955), 131; *Gesammelte Werke* (Frankfurt a. M.: S. Fischer, 1968), 16:210 (hereafter *GW*). Further page numbers will be given in the body of the text, first to the English, then to the German edition.

4. The German phrase is even stranger when read literally, since the verb, *schaffen*, designates making or creating: *creatio* not *ex nihilo* but *in nihilum*. It is also Freud's preferred expression in describing Moses' relation to the Jews.

5. *GW* 16:213. Freud even asserts that "we know, that behind the God, who chose the Jews and freed them from Egypt, stands the person of Moses" (ibid.).

6. *GW* 14:218.

7. "In the face of new persecutions, one once again has to ask how the Jew has become what he is and why he attracts such eternal hatred. I have found the following formula: Moses created the Jew and my work will have as its title, *Moses: A Historical Novel* . . ." (Sigmund Freud, cited in Michel de Certeau, *L'Écriture de l'histoire* [Paris: Gallimard, 1975], 314).

8. Given that he was writing in the years between 1936 and 1939, Freud's persistent use of the word *Führer* in these essays can hardly be separated from the National Socialist Führer cult. (The same would not hold true for his use of the word in *Mass Psychology and Ego Analysis*, written in the early twenties.) If Freud retains this highly charged word in the later essay, it is perhaps to provoke reflection on the possible significance of this relationship. Notwithstanding his enormous respect for Moses, Freud does not hesitate to designate him as a "tyrant" (see *Moses and Monotheism*, 58), however "spiritual" and "ethical" the religion he brought to, or "imposed" on, the Jewish people. The relationship between the two instances of *Führer*, if it exists, is extremely complex and would require long and nuanced analysis, which cannot be attempted here.

9. In a prefatory note, the translator, Katherine Jones, states that she "had the advantage of consulting the author on some doubtful points" (Freud, *Moses and Monotheism*, 2). She does not, however, mention whether this title was one of them.

10. Toward the conclusion of a recent essay, "The Right of the Strongest: Are There Rogue States?," Jacques Derrida returns to the often-quoted assertion made by Heidegger in his posthumously published interview with the German newsmagazine *Der Spiegel*: "Nothing but a God can save us." Derrida points out that "Heidegger says 'a god' (*un dieu, ein Gott*), not the One God (*le Dieu Un*)," noting that "*a* god is neither *one* God nor *many* Gods. What interests me above all here is this difference in number" (Jacques Derrida, *Voyous*, [Paris: Galilée, 2003], 156). I will return to this question of number, and to the difference between "one" and "a," which is condensed in the "indefinite article," at the end of this text.

11. Freud quotes one of his most important scholarly sources, Edward Meyer, to the effect that "the name *Mose* is probably . . . Egyptian." But Meyer continues, "That does not prove, of course, that these tribes were of Egyptian origin, but only that they stood in relation to Egypt." To which Freud responds: "One can ask, to be sure, just what sort of relations one is to imagine" (*Moses and Monotheism*, 14/112n.).

12. From whom, however, he borrows more than he indicates, including the notion alluded to at the end of the passage just quoted, namely, that the messianic hope which led to Christianity evolved in response to the guilt that resulted from the murder of the founding prophet by his people. See Ernst Sellin, *Mose und seine Bedeutung für die israelitisch-jüdische Religionsgeschichte* (Leipzig: A. Deichert, 1911), 124.

13. Freud's relation to his authoritative scholarly predecessors—here, Sellin—displays the same ambivalence that he finds in the relation of son to father: on the one hand, the recognition of an uncontested authority; on the other, the dismissal or at least limitation of that authority. It is as if such authority—or, as Freud puts it, "authors"—were necessary, but primarily in order to be dismissed. The word that Freud uses in this context, *glaubwürdig*—trustworthy or, more literally, worthy of belief—is thus the expression of a relation of extreme ambivalence, which perhaps explains at least in part what Freud later in the essay designates "the altogether mysterious emotional phenomenon of belief" ("ganz rätselhaften emotionellen Phänomen des Glaubens"; 151/226).

14. Although for Freud, of course, memories can themselves be a form of forgetting, as with so-called "screen memories" (in German, *Deckerinnerungen*).

15. For this reason, I would prefer to translate Kafka's title as *The Man Who Went Missing* rather than *The Man Who Disappeared*.

16. Sigmund Freud, *Totem and Taboo* (New York: Norton), 176; *GW* 9:171–72. Further page numbers will be given in the text.

17. *GW* 14:140.

18. *GW* 14:151. Although Freud does not mention it, in German there is a close association between the process of "concentrating" and that of *Ausblendung*: that is, excluding distracting associations. From this point of view, "free association" could be defined as the re-inclusion, the *Wiedereinblendung* of that which has been excluded from consciousness in the process of concentrating or "focusing" on an object. On the question of "isolation," see Samuel Weber, *The Legend of Freud*, 2d ed. (Stanford: Stanford University Press, 2002), 95–96.

19. *GW* 14:151.

20. See my discussion of the role of "binding" in ego formation and its relation to language in *The Legend of Freud*, 75–85.

5. Networks, Netwar, and Narratives

1. Admiral Arthur K. Cebrowski, in "An Interview with the Director," August 2002, http://216.239.59.104/search?q=cache:VLVQzbmtBUgJ:www.oft.osd.mil/library/library_files/trends_164_transformation_trends_28_october_issue.pd f+Arthur+Cebrowski+Interview+with+the+Director&hl=en.

2. http://www.whitehouse/gov/nsc/print/nssall.html, 7, 15.

3. Attachment to "Creationism" remains one of the strongest arti-

cles of faith for the Christian Right, which forms a powerful constituency of the Bush administration. According to a poll taken in 1999, 79 percent of Americans felt that Creationism should be taught in public schools (http://www.umass.edu/journal/450/creationism/poll_origin_theories.html).

4. That task has indeed "changed dramatically" today, not least by virtue of this declaration itself. Though President Bush asserts that "defending our Nation" is the "first and fundamental commitment of the Federal Government," the Preamble to the Constitution upon which his government is based places the establishment of "Justice" *before* all other objectives, *including those of national security*: "We the People of the United States, in Order to form a more perfect Union, *establish Justice*, insure domestic Tranquility, provide for the common defense, promote the general Welfare, and secure the Blessings of Liberty to ourselves and our Posterity, do ordain and establish this Constitution for the United States of America" (my italics). The formation of "a more perfect Union" thus seems predicated, first and foremost, upon the establishment of *justice*. According to the Constitution, then, considerations of national security should be informed by considerations of justice rather than the other way round. To "justify" the reversal of these priorities "today," which is to say, in the post–cold war world, an atmosphere of fear and crisis has to be sustained. It is this reversal that defines the dominant political function in the United States of the attacks of September 11, 2001. This interpretation or presentation of "9–11" as the inauguration of a state of permanent exception (*Ausnahmezustand*) differs radically from that prevalent in other parts of the world and contributes to the growing gap between public policy and opinion in the United States and that of the rest of the world.

5. Bush speech, 1, my emphasis.

6. One increasingly used phrase that suggests the tenor of this phenomenon is the often-stressed need to "move forward" and not remain mired in the mud of history.

7. Zbigniew Brzezinski, *The Grand Chessboard: American Primacy and Its Geostrategic Imperatives* (New York: Basic Books, 1998).

8. Zbigniew Brzezinski, quoted in John Pilger, "The Warlords of America," http://www.informationclearinghouse.info/article6777.-htm. Brzezinski's critique of the use to which his ideas were put by the "neo-conservative" policies of the second Bush administration are thus indicative of a difference, not in ultimate geopolitical objectives, but rather in the strategy by which they can best be attained. As John Pilger remarks, "It was the liberal Carter, not Reagan, that laid the ground for George W. Bush."

9. Mike Davis, "Slouching Toward Baghdad . . ." Znet Foreign Policy, http://www.zmag.org/content/showarticle.cfm?SectionID=11&ItemID=3150.

10. Ibid.

11. Arthur K. Cebrowski and John J. Garstka, "Network-Centric Warfare: Its Origin and Future," Naval Institute Proceedings, 1998, http://www.usni.org/Proceedings/Articles98/PROcebrowski.htm.

12. John Arquilla and David Ronfeldt, *Networks and Netwars* (Santa Monica, Calif.: Rand, 2001). Future references will appear in the body of the text.

13. Ibid., 9, my emphasis.

14. Experience of the past decades has demonstrated that the difference between these two groups is in practice hardly as clear-cut as conventional wisdom has it.

15. "The boundaries of the network, or of any node included in it, may be well-defined, or blurred and porous in relation to the outside environment" (Arquilla and Ronfeldt, *Networks and Netwars*, 8).

16. Walter Benjamin, *Ursprung des deutschen Trauerspiels*, *Gesammelte Schriften*, vol. 1 (Frankfurt a. M.: Suhrkamp, 1980).

17. Ibid., 351.

18. Ibid., 364.

19. "Without" here—as Derrida has shown of the Kantian suffix *-los* (as in "interesse*loses* Wohlgefallen," pleasure without interest)—marks, not the negation or abrogation of a relationship, but its irreducible exteriority and alterity. See Jacques Derrida, "Le Sans de la coupure pure," *La Vérité en peinture* (Paris: Flammarion, 1978), 95–135.

20. Walter Benjamin, "Der Erzähler," *Gesammelte Schriften,* 2.2:457.

21. Ibid., 455.

22. Ibid., 453.

23. Ibid., 454.

24. It is difficult here not to hear the echoes of the Nazi slogan "Ein Reich—ein Volk—ein Führer!"

6. The Net and the Carpets

1. Walter Benjamin, "Der Erzähler," *Gesammelte Schriften* (Frankfurt a. M.: Suhrkamp, 1980), 2.2:453. (Hereafter *GS*.)

2. *GS* 6:100–103.

3. Walter Benjamin, *Selected Writings*, vol. 1, *1913–26*, ed. Marcus Bullock and Michael W. Jennings (Cambridge: Harvard University

Press, 1996), 288–91. Further references to this edition will be given in the body of the text, with pages of the English edition preceding those of the German original.

4. The English translation repeats what is clearly an error in the German edition, first noted by Uwe Steiner ("Kapitalismus als Religion: Anmerkungen zu einem Fragment Walter Benjamins," *Deutsche Vierteljahresschrift* 72 (1998), vol. 1, 157n.25). The German edition reads, "sans *rêve* et merci," "without *dream* or mercy" (*GS* 1:288). Although Benjamin was fascinated by dreams, he would never have made their *absence* a defining characteristic of capitalism. As the context makes clear, the word *dream* here makes little sense, for what Benjamin is asserting is the *unremitting* and *merciless* tempo of the capitalist cult, whether seen from the side of production or from that of consumption.. Benjamin would have known the French expression from Baudelaire's poem "Le Crépuscule du soir," one of the *Tableaux Parisiens*, which he had been translating for years, a translation he completed in the same year that he wrote "Capitalism as Religion." The phrase is decisive for the poem, which recounts how the evening twilight in Paris no longer functions as a refuge and consolation from the burdens of a day that for most is a workday. Evening brings no "truce" to the weary, for no sooner has the sun begun to set than sinister figures emerge to prey upon them.

5. One cannot but think here of President Schreber, who, although he avoids using the word *guilt* in his *Memoirs* (D. P. Schreber, *Denkwürdigekeiten eines Nervenkranken* [Berlin: Ullstein, 1973]), nevertheless describes how God, driven by the "desire" for "constant enjoyment" ("verlangt . . . beständiges Geniessen," 293), falls progressively under the "attraction" of Schreber's "nerves." The desire for uninterrupted and perennial enjoyment makes the deity dependent upon human finitude, so that Schreber is convinced that his death cannot but have serious consequences for God (300). This concern is inseparable from what Schreber describes as the "egoism of God" (355). Divine egoism drives the deity to commit or sanction violence against his own creation, described by Schreber as "soul murder": through this act, Schreber speculates, God "chained Himself to an individual human being," thus exposing Himself both to the attractive power of the latter's "nerves" and to the limitations of human existence. Because of the threat such limitations pose to divine transcendence, God resists this attraction with "the most extreme and ruthless cruelty" (355). The result is a situation of hostility and struggle that violates the "world order" but also, Schreber is convinced,

can lead, after his death, thus rendered sacrificial, to its ultimate triumph (356). Many features of this ambivalent configuration are to be found in the world dominated by the religious "cult of capitalism" as Benjamin describes it. Schreber can thus be considered one of its high priests.

6. *GS* 1.1:308ff.

7. *GS* 1.1:504.

8. *Selected Writings*, 1:203.

9. "Law [*Das Recht*] condemns not to punishment but to guilt. Destiny is the guilt-nexus [*Schuldzusammenhang*] of the living" (*GS* 2.1:175, 204).

10. *GS* 6:101. The English translation misreads *Reife*, which it renders as "immaturity," *Unreife* (*Selected Writings*, 1:289).

11. Friedrich Hölderlin, "Anmerkungen zur Antigonä," *Hölderlin: Werke und Briefe*, ed. F. Beißner and Jochen Schmidt (Frankfurt a. M.: Suhrkamp, 1969), 2:789.

12. Walter Benjamin, "Zwei Gedichte von Friedrich Hölderlin," *GS* 2.1:105–26; "Two Poems by Friedrich Hölderlin," *Selected Writings*, 1:18–36. Future references will be given in the body of the text, first to the English, then to the German pagination. The root of the German title of Hölderlin's poem, "Blödigkeit," *blöd*, comes from the Middle High German *bloede*, meaning "fragile, weak, tender, erratic," and from Old High German *blodi*, "unknowing, shy, fearful." It is related to *bloß*, "bare" (*Duden Herkunftswörterbuch* [Mannheim: Duden, 1963], 73).

13. The excellent English translation of Stanley Corngold uses Emerson's term "poetized." I prefer to use the more familiar "poeticized," since it retains the meaning "to put into poetry" (OED), which I take to correspond fairly closely to Benjamin's use of *das Gedichtete*.

14. "Determinacy" would of course be a more idiomatic translation, but I agree with Corngold's translation since it is important to retain the notion that the "poeticized" is capable of being determined rather than already determined, as "determinacy" would imply. The awkwardness of "determinability" is the necessary price to pay for this precision.

15. See chapter 4, above.

16. Jean-Luc Nancy, *Être singulier pluriel* (Paris: Galilée, 1996); *Being Singular Plural*, trans. Robert D. Richardson and Anne E. O'Byrne (Stanford: Stanford University Press, 2000).

17. Cf. Fr. Nietzsche, *The Birth of Tragedy*, §25: "Could we think

how dissonance becomes human? [*eine Menschwerdung der Dissonanz*]—and what else is man?'' Benjamin's reading of Hölderlin stages ''dissonance becoming an image'' rather than ''human,'' for only via the mediation of the image is the ''dissonance'' transposed into the sphere of the ''living.'' Benjamin cites the Nietzschean phrase in his *Origins of the German Mourning Play*, *GS* 1.1:282.

18. Cf. W. Benjamin, *The Origins of the German Mourning Play*, chap. 3.

Index